Reclaiming My Life

my Journey Back to God

Second Edition

Nick Nicholas

Publication information:
Reclaiming My Life: my Journey Back to God (second Edition)
ISBN: 978-1-998014-31-6
Copyright © 2024 Nick Nicholas

Print Editing and Layout and e-pub creation:
I. Gaudet, Success Publications

Published by:
Success Publications – division of Creativity Corner Inc.
Box 10, Egremont, AB T0A 0Z0
www.SuccessPublications.ca

Foreword
April 1992 – Powder Springs, GA

I slowly opened my eyes as I awoke and saw the sunlight shining through the blinds and across my bed. I smelled the sweet spring air flowing through the open window. I felt refreshed, aware of a deep sense that something was significantly different. I'd never felt this way. My body felt light as a feather, and I was tingling with excitement bordering on euphoria. As I sat up, I shouted, "Oh my God, this is a feeling that no one will ever be able to take away from me. This truly is the first day of the rest of my life."

I was screaming and laughing at the same time. Had my wife been in the house, she would have thought I was crazy.

What was this feeling I was experiencing? Was it real or imagined? Was it temporary or permanent? Then gently it settled into my conscious mind that this feeling was real; it was a deep lasting peace, the kind of peace that makes life heaven on earth. It's the peace that finally – in my troubled life – gave understanding to the words Jesus said to his disciples, *"Peace I leave with you; my peace I give you."* (John 14:27 NIV)

I realized that the peace I was experiencing was from God. But what I had not yet realized was that the adversity I would continue to face was

God's way of helping me to strengthen my spiritual self, which, I believe, is the main reason he put me on this earth. Furthermore, it became very clear to me as life went on, that achieving ultimate peace is a journey not a destination.

Years of experience taught me that life does not allow peace to remain stagnant. Adversity will force it to grow stronger or be destroyed. For example, a couple deeply in love feels peace between them. However, life's everyday challenges attempt to erode that peace because the fear of those challenges weakens the relationship over time.

In my experience only fear can destroy peace. I have learned that the only way that I can maintain and grow the peace that I felt that beautiful morning is to master the fears I face everyday. I now know that I have a choice. I will control fear or fear will control me. I will elaborate on this later.

My purpose is twofold. First, I want to share with you how to overcome fear to achieve spiritual peace. Secondly, I want you to share it. I believe that once we have learned to achieve peace in our lives, we have a responsibility to pass it on to others. In so doing, one person at a time, we can bring peace to families, communities, and countries.

I know that many people feel confused, frustrated and even angry about where they are in

4

life. So, if you are experiencing any of these feelings, you may be wondering how you can overcome them and find peace. Let me share with you experiences from my journey, which may help you on your personal quest for peace.

Chapter 1

I grew up in a small farm town in Southeast Kansas. The early years were very good for me. Unfortunately, my mother and biological father divorced when I was three years old. My mother remarried, and she and my stepfather taught me the importance of faith based on a belief in God. They also taught me a good work ethic, strong values, and morality. I learned the difference between right and wrong, and that doing what was good brought positive rewards, while doing wrong brought punishment.

Yes, I grew up in the days when the punishment you got for fighting in school was nothing compared to the punishment you would get when you got home. There was no blaming others. You were clearly responsible for your own actions. I practiced what I was taught, and my life was based on a deep faith in God.

In June of 1958, my faith was challenged for the first time when my mother died unexpectedly between my junior and senior year of high school. I was devastated because I thought I'd done what was right. I worked hard and helped others. So why was God punishing me? Then, less than five weeks later, I discovered that the girl I'd been dating since my sophomore year – who I loved very much – was not who I thought she was. I learned that she was involved in intimate relationships with several of my closest friends. My heart was broken. At that point, I doubted my faith in myself, and my faith in God.

I didn't realize it then, but this was a major turning point in my life, which became the pattern for years to come. I was angry, bitter, and resentful. Those negative feelings would remain attached to me for many years, repressed, but fully charged. Even though I might have appeared content on the outside, shadows of negativity colored my attitude about life in general.

By the time I got to college in September 1959, I'd decided that maybe there wasn't such a clear-cut line between right and wrong. Yes, I now saw gray. Maybe it's not right, but maybe it's not totally wrong either. Rules were made to be bent to a particular situation, especially when it got me what I wanted. Why not? Others were doing it, and they didn't seem to suffer any negative consequences. Obviously, I was drifting from my Christian roots.

My first year of college in Pittsburg, KS, was a lot of fun. I got to do things that I'd been taught were wrong. But now they fit very nicely into varying shades of gray that had become my new morality. I discovered that a college campus was full of great looking woman, many of whom were looking to broaden more than just their intellectual disciplines. In high school, except for the girl I thought I was in love with, I had five dates in four years. In college I found I could have a different date every night if I wanted. Meanwhile, I discovered that women found me attractive and charming, something I had never experienced previously. Therefore, I was out to enjoy everything I thought I had missed in high school.

It was party time, and I was ready to party with a vengeance. I was focused on two main objectives. Number one was to party and enjoy life. Number two was to make enough money to support my new lifestyle. So, I worked at a small restaurant across the street from the campus. This gave me the opportunity to earn money, eat free, and meet women. Unfortunately, I was having so much fun I ignored the fact that I was there to get an education. Consequently, after reviewing my grades, the college informed me that I could not re-enroll for the next semester.

I didn't really mind though, because I'd met a wonderful woman in psychology class, and we were married that summer. I was eighteen years old. Over the next eight years we had two wonderful children. I had secured a great job with a large insurance company as an account manager for several major corporations. That position came with a great salary, a company car, an expense account, and bonuses. Life was great. This was the American dream, and I was beginning to think that my lack of faith in God was not a mistake. Some of my internal conflicts began to subside. At this time, we were living in Erie, KS.

Then I came face to face with the cold hard facts of life. I was twenty-six when I discovered that my wife was having an affair with my best friend. I blew up and she filed for divorce. What was it about the women in my life and my best friends? My thoughts kept returning to the question, what's wrong with me, as a man, that women can't be faithful to me? What am I lacking? It had to be me since this wasn't my first rodeo. Maybe it's better not to have friends, male or female, I thought.

It was then I decided to never let anyone get close to me. I'd take what I wanted from the relationship and move on. Did I hurt a few people? Yes, I did. But in my mind, it was simply justifiable self-protection. My motto became, "Do unto others BEFORE they have a chance to DO UNTO YOU." At that point in time, fear ran my life. I didn't know it at the time. But I was running scared.

So, with a pending divorce, a cheating wife, a badly damaged sense of self-worth – and no family to turn to – I lost the will to fight. I turned in my company car, quit my job, and disappeared into the homeless community. I felt hopeless. Because of family circumstances, my stepmother and father chose to support my wife in the divorce. My stepfather had passed away five years earlier. The situation left me with very limited interaction with my children. I saw no light at the end of the tunnel. I was gripped by fear for my survival. My life was a dark hole with no foreseeable future. Only years later would I understand that God had allowed this to happen to prepare me to master the very fear that was threatening my life at that time. God impressed upon me that no matter what happened to me, He was always preparing me for my mission in life.

At this point, my internal conflicts were killing me. My thoughts wandered back to when I had gotten my first job. I was in the 7th grade when there were no rules against children working in small farm communities. My parents sat me down and explained that it was critical that I do my best and always go the extra mile. I always stayed busy and looked for more to do because my actions and my reputation reflected on the family name and affected the family's reputation in the community. I'd been taught that when things got tough, you persevered; you got up, dusted yourself off, and moved on. This time, however, I just didn't give a damn. I was overwhelmed with anger, jealousy, and the injustice of the whole episode. I had done nothing wrong. Yet again I felt punished for the actions of others.

Leaving wasn't going to reflect well on my reputation or that of the family. As I said before, I'd been taught that doing what was right earned me rewards and that doing wrong earned me punishments. Now I was deeply conflicted because I'd been trying my best to do good, being a productive member of society providing for a family, while others were doing wrong.

Hey God! What's wrong with this picture? How about a little help here! Unfortunately, I didn't see any. How screwed up is that?

Sorry God, no more faith. I'm on my own now. I ended up spending most of my time in Parsons, KS, because it was larger than Erie, where everyone knew me. In Parsons, I found it easier to avoid people I knew. I was humiliated by what had happened.

Then I discovered that I wasn't as alone as I'd thought. I had a talent for getting people to like me and to volunteer to help me. They gave me periodic donations that allowed me to buy food or alcohol, usually alcohol first, and to pay for a warm place to stay. Occasionally a woman would offer to let me stay with her for a few days. Other times, I knew several local bartenders who allowed me to sleep in their storerooms if the weather was exceedingly bad. This unfortunately, wasn't always the case. At times, I slept outside.

Four days before Thanksgiving in 1968, I woke up in an alley in downtown Joplin, MO. I

11

was freezing cold, starving, and sporting the mother of all hangovers. I got to my feet and went looking for some coffee. As I walked around the corner of a large building, I noticed that it was a federal building. I knew that some offices in that building would be open and have the coffee that I so desperately needed.

I stumbled through the door and followed the wonderful smell into the only open office. It was the U.S. Army recruiting office. That day I got a lot more than a cup of coffee. That day, my life took a hard-right turn. It was years later that I realized that joining the Army was the first step on my long road back to God. The next day, I was on a bus heading to Fort Leonard Wood, MO.

Chapter 2

Ask anyone who's ever been in the military about his first day of basic training. He'll tell you it's an experience that he will remember for as long as he lives. Mine was no different. As we got off the bus in our company area, I swear that every Drill Sergeant in the Army greeted us. They were screaming, calling us every name you could imagine, many of which I'd never heard. I was only a foot or so from the door of the barracks when a Drill Sergeant stopped me, screaming, asking me if I knew how many snaps were on my field jacket.

I said, "No" and he screamed that there were 10 as he unsnapped each one. Then he told me that they were to be snapped at all times. Since mine were not in regulation, I owed him 10 pushups for each one. Even in my frazzled state, I knew that was 100 pushups. To say that I was not in good physical shape would have been a great understatement. I dropped and pushed out 20. I was so weak I couldn't do any more. I fell to the ground saying, "I can't do anymore."

Now let me tell you that in my life I've made mistakes. But this one was burned into my brain forever. The Drill Sergeant jerked me off the ground like I weighed nothing. Holding me with one hand, he slapped me across the face so hard that I saw stars, and my partial came loose and flipped around inside my mouth like a lawnmower blade. Yes, that was back in the time when you could instill discipline and responsibility in a soldier without asking his permission.

The Sergeant's face was nearly purple and the veins in his neck were standing like steel cords as he screamed, "Can't! Can't! Listen to me you maggot, there is no such word as can't. That word no longer exists in your vocabulary. It has been replaced by 'will!' *'I can't'* is for wimps, *'I will'* is for men." With that he threw me back on the ground and I gave him 80 more pushups. It is amazing what adrenaline can do for your strength. Later that day, four others and I were selected as trainee leaders for the training cycle.

I'll not go into detail how we were selected, suffice to say that we all had sore jaws and small traces of blood in the corners of our mouths. Nevertheless, we were bonded in a way I'd never experienced. I had found a new family, one that I respected, and which respected me in return. We trusted each other and we had each other's back. The training was grueling, and the winter weather in Missouri is anything but pleasant. I swear I was never warm the entire time I was there. I've heard many who were stationed there refer to Ft. Leonard Wood as little Korea. It was a long ten weeks, but I felt pride in completing my training.

The morning of graduation we were all excited. We'd survived. We'd learned a lot and grown a lot more. I entered the Army as a 126-pound weakling. Now I weighed 175 pounds, mostly muscle. I had a great six-pack and an attitude that I could conquer the world. Now it was time for the next phase of training. I was looking forward to it.

But the celebration was bittersweet. Mail call came that morning just before we marched off to the graduation ceremony. I got a bit of a surprise. My Drill Sergeant, the one who taught me about *"can't"* passed out the mail. He called me front and center. Looking me in the eye, he handed me a large envelope saying, "I want to present you with your final divorce decree. See me immediately after the ceremony."

That gut punch dampened my excitement and left me with mixed feelings. First, I felt a deep sadness because I still loved my ex-wife. Second, I felt anger. My primary thought was, just you wait bitch, I'll show you what you gave up. Anger motivated me from that point for many years. I wanted to prove that I was a better man.

After the ceremony, my Drill Sergeant took me and the other trainee leaders to a bar to celebrate. He wouldn't let me spend a dime. He kept feeding me drinks. At one point, he leaned over to me and said, "Remember, *'I can't'* is for wimps. *'I will'* is for men. Never look back.

Always look forward. You are definitely a man now."

I will admit that, to this day, I have no memory of leaving that bar, or of my military flight to Fort Lewis, WA. My next conscious memory was of being in formation watching a huge Samoan drill sergeant doing 100 pushups with his right hand, and then switching and doing 100 more on his left hand. The message was 'don't mess with me'. Yep, I got it, message received.

After my infantry training and some special training, I got what I wanted since I'd joined the army – orders for Vietnam. Then something happened that I later realize was just one more turning point in my journey back to God. My orders were changed, and I was sent to Warrant Officer Flight School in Fort Wolters, TX, for helicopter flight training.

I thought I'd learned all there was to know about harassment and humiliation until I entered my first four weeks of flight school as a "Snowbird". I'll not bore you with the details. Suffice to say that I saw more than one man drop to his knees crying, begging to leave the program because of the psychological pressure. The great news is that I got PhD-level training in leadership and paying attention to detail, which is critical for any pilot.

Before I joined the Army, I had experienced periods of extreme anxiety, and I had suffered at least two panic attacks. I really believed, though, that after my military training and with my current level of self-confidence, that my panic attacks were a thing of the past. But I was wrong and discovered this at the worst possible time, while I was flying solo. I had flown solo before with no problem. But this flight was very different. It was a beautiful morning. The sun was shining. The temperature was perfect with little or no wind – a perfect day for flying.

Suddenly, from out of nowhere, I felt a deep sense of fear. Then I suffered one of the most severe panic attacks I'd ever had. Now let me say that having a panic attack while flying solo at 1500 feet in a helicopter is not an ideal situation. If you've ever had a panic attack, you know that the only thing you consider is getting to a safe place. Yes, I had to get out of the air and onto the ground.

So, I headed for the stage field. There are procedures and protocols for taking off and landing any aircraft. But on this day, they meant nothing to me at all. I wanted to be on the ground NOW! I flew through the traffic pattern without regard for other aircraft. My radio exploded with expletives from the tower and from other pilots. That didn't matter. I was going to land regardless of regulations.

Finally, I landed on an active runway, but didn't clear off the runway. I just sat there shaking. Other aircraft were aborting, and the air traffic controller was screaming at me to clear! But for me it was finally over, for the time being. Obviously, deep-seated fear had caused the panic attack. At that moment, I didn't try to find the cause. I wouldn't even have known where to look. But I was to learn years later that the fear would return again and again until I decided to acknowledge and overcome it.

Not surprisingly, the Army decided that I probably wouldn't be a good pilot and chose to reassign me. I was told to fill out my dream sheet. If you are current or former military, you are familiar with a dream sheet. If you're not, it is a list of your top three wishes for assignment. In my opinion, it is the military's way of eliminating those options in selecting your next assignment.

I listed infantry Vietnam as all three choices. So, in its infinite wisdom, command assigned me to Air Defense Artillery, which was learning to operate the Nike Hercules Missile System. I was disappointed and angry. I wanted to go to Vietnam and be the combat soldier I was trained to be. Like any good soldier, however, I followed orders and tried to be the best soldier I could be wherever the Army placed me. At least that part of my upbringing had not abandoned me.

Chapter 3

My next two years in the Air Defense Artillery Command went quickly. Quite honestly, I found it to be rather boring, except for the fact that I was married for a second time. I'd known her for many years before I enlisted in the Army. I had decided that for my own preservation, I needed to settle down. At 29, my constant drinking and womanizing was taking a major toll on my health. She was divorced with three children. Now I had a family, which in some ways replaced the family from my first marriage. If you're wondering, I was allowed limited contact with my two biological children.

When the Army shut down the Nike Hercules Missile System, I was reassigned to the Army Recruiting Command, an assignment that most career Non-Commissioned Officers (NCOs) dreaded.

It's important for you to understand that from the time I left flight school until the end of my assignment to the Air Defense Command, I struggled hard to overcome my feelings of personal failure. I kept thinking I'd failed at my high school romance. I'd failed in my marriage. I'd failed my father and myself when I didn't complete flight school. In my mind I was a complete failure.

These constant thoughts of failure led me to realize that I needed a stable life with a loving relationship. Even though I was not happy in my second marriage, I felt that it was necessary to make the best of it because I wanted to focus on my career and try to be a good husband and a good soldier.

Now my life would stabilize, and we'd live happily ever after, right? Wrong! Within a few days after the marriage, I knew I'd made a big mistake. I'd made the decision to marry for all the wrong reasons. It's not that I didn't have feelings for her. I did. But they were not the deep feelings of love necessary to sustain a happy, long-lasting marriage.

The truth is that my decision to marry a second time was based on the fear of being alone more than it was on love and trust. I also didn't want to disappoint my mother and stepfather, who had raised me to be loyal to my wife and family. Like many people, I was trying to live up to my parents' standards. Even though they were deceased, they were still a part of how I made my decisions and lived my life. No question, this created enormous internal conflict in me.

Unfortunately, my wife and I clashed, and we found ourselves constantly bickering and fighting. She wanted to be the directing force in the marriage, and I resisted strongly. It didn't go well. But we stayed together for 13 years. What's the old saying? "You made your bed. Now lay in it." The problem was this: I was still being motivated by my anger toward my first wife. I wanted to show her that I was a success, even it if meant staying in a bad marriage.

Moreover, because of living out of my past, I had a very low opinion of women in general. Therefore, I was not a good husband. In fact, I began drinking more and more, trying to kill the emotional pain, which eventually led me to start cheating, and before long, we were leading separate miserable lives.

As I look back, I now understand the increased drinking and cheating was my way of trying to kill the pain caused by my emotional stress. What I came to realize was that emotional pain was significantly worse than physical pain. Physical pain is recognized and treated, while emotional pain is often denied or misdiagnosed, leading the individual to self-medicate using alcohol, drugs, sex, overeating, etc. It seems we can easily justify these actions, and we are not usually questioned about them.

My upbringing told me that you follow the Ten Commandants, including not committing adultery. My parents taught me to do nothing to excess. Now here I was, doing exactly the opposite, which in psychological terms is called cognitive dissonance. I'll tell you it doesn't make any difference what it's called; it kept my life in a constant state of chaos.

For anyone who might be in this situation, let me say this, the saying that what she doesn't know won't hurt her is a myth. The truth is best described by the words of a country song, *"What she don't know won't hurt her, but it's destroying me."* You can recognize it and fix it, or you can do as I did; I lied to myself. I told myself how much fun I was having when I was miserable. I had convinced myself that my ability to drink, seduce women (undetected I might add), and support a family made me superman.

So now I'm a proud member of the U.S. Army's Recruiting Command. As I said earlier, most career NCOs dreaded this assignment. In my case, I loved it. I'd been in sales before my world exploded in my face and had been successful. Suddenly, I realized that I was not a complete professional failure. I excelled at recruiting. Ironically, my first duty station was in the federal building where I had enlisted in Joplin, MO, five years before on that cold November morning. Even with all the turmoil in my life, I felt better about myself than I did five years before, which gave me some hope for the future.

My career continued to grow, and after four years as a field recruiter, I was reassigned to the Army's recruiting school at Fort Benjamin Harrison, IN. Wow! For me this was the jewel of all assignments. Being an instructor came naturally to me. Life was great, at least professionally. Personally, it was miserable. I was still drinking and cheating. My stress levels were going off the chart as the gap between what I was doing and what I had been taught to do was growing wider and wider. In fact, three times I experienced alcohol poisoning and had to be taken to the hospital. On my third visit, I got the same doctor as I had the previous two. Fort Benjamin Harrison is a small installation that only had a few doctors at the time. I just lucked out and got the same one all three times. In his direct military bedside manner, he explained my situation.

"Sarge," he said angrily, "This is your third strike; I'll help you this time because I don't have time to do all the paperwork to explain your death. But if it happens again, don't bother to come in here and waste my time, just crawl into a gutter and die. If you feel you must come here, I'll put you on a gurney in the hallway and let you die there. Do you get my message?"

God, I love military doctors. Truly I do, because they call a spade a spade and that is important in life. I didn't quit drinking, but I damn sure backed off a lot.

At the end of my four years at the recruiting school, I was reassigned to the Kansas City Recruiting Battalion, taking my wife, the three

23

children, and my constant misery with me. Then it happened, the foreshadowing of the traumatic events I was to experience over the next several years. Some would be bad, some good, but all of them would be totally life changing. The emotional roller coaster I was about to ride was like nothing I could have imagined. In short, these events would put me on the final leg of my journey back home to God.

It had only been a few months since leaving the recruiting school, and being assigned back to the battalion, when my life took a seismic shift, somewhere near a nine on the Richter scale. Because of my reputation as an instructor and training designer, I was sent back to the recruiting school on a temporary basis for a period of 90 days. I was ecstatic. I'd be back to doing what I loved and would be away from my wife for three months.

I know, that wasn't the right attitude. But by this time, I'd hardened my heart to the point that I was not the man who my parents had raised me to be. In fact, I didn't even know who that person was. Professionally I had grown. Personally, I was an emotional wreck on the inside. Everyone thought that I had my life together. It was a lie. Honestly, I had recently made up my mind that my life was basically a shell. I felt like I had already died inside and was only waiting for the physical death to arrive. I'd convinced myself that

I wouldn't live beyond the age of my mother when she died at 52.

So off I went to have three months of freedom and fun. Surely that would keep my emotional pain at bay for a while. Because of the large influx of NCOs and officers to be trained, there was no billeting on base. So, instructors and students from some of the other classes were put up in a local motel.

On the Monday morning of my third week, I was sitting in the dining room with several other NCOs that I knew. When I looked up, there stood the most beautiful strawberry blond I'd ever seen. She was wearing an Army uniform, which she filled out perfectly. I immediately thought there was my next conquest. I didn't hesitate for a second. I got up and gave her my seat at the table. God, what was that all about? I was so attracted to her that I forgot the fact that she was an NCO. This was very unusual because I was treating her as a woman rather than as an NCO. I wasn't supposed to treat her differently because of her gender.

I saw her several times in passing over the next few days. Then one evening, after working late, I went into the dining room to grab a hamburger to take to my room. I then went into the lounge to get a beer. Someone called out my name, and as I looked around, I saw a friend of mine in a booth. He was sitting with another

NCO. Across from them sat my beautiful strawberry blond. I took my beer over and sat down next to her. As I sat down, there was a very strong electrical spark between us. In fact, it was strong enough that both guys noticed it and commented about it.

Before I left, I asked her out for pizza and a movie. She accepted. I was on cloud nine because my seduction plan was right on schedule. I could hardly wait. But the night did not go according to plan probably because I was nervous. In addition, there was something different about this woman. She was not like my other conquests. She exuded a quiet confidence, a strong sense of purpose, and was not to be manipulated.

There's a country song, *"Lonely Women Make Good Lovers."* From my experience this was true. When I was on the run, that's who I was looking for. However, every signal I received from Darlene said that this description did not fit her in any way. Truthfully, I was scared to death of a long-term relationship because I never had a good one and didn't believe it could happen for me. Looking back, I now realize I had already started falling in love with this beautiful and unique woman.

The night we went out for pizza we saw the movie *"Honeysuckle Rose,"* about a country band starring Willie Nelson. I loved it since I'd played in a small country band previously and always enjoyed it. Afterwards, we went back to my motel room to talk and enjoy each other's company. I was deeply conflicted because I wanted to get her in bed. At the same time, I wanted to go slower and get to know her. Unlike my previous encounters, it was important that she feel totally comfortable and would be willing to go out with me again.

Nevertheless, my drive to seduce took over and we began making out. But the moment I tried to go further she stopped me cold, telling me she did not want to get involved because she had just ended a bad relationship. She wanted companionship. She let me know in no uncertain terms that 'no' meant 'no'. This was something I was not accustomed to. As we sat there looking at each other, I realized that something had changed in me. I just didn't know what had changed. I tried half-heartedly to change her mind because I still wanted an immediate, intimate relationship with her. But she would not have anything to do with it.

At this point, I gave up on my seduction plan and began to share my story with her. Curious, she began asking me questions about my life. So, I began to share intimate thoughts with her. With that came the story of heartbreak, betrayal, and failure. She listened to all my sadness, my feelings of failure, and much more. By early morning I had told her things that I'd never told anyone, much less admitted to myself.

I'd never felt more comfortable talking to anyone in my life. For some reason, I felt I could trust her. To this day I believe that God was talking to me through her. As she spoke, I began to see a glimmer of hope and at least the possibility of a brighter future.

As she started asking me questions about my life, I was encouraged to open up because she did not judge me, talk down to me, or condemn me. By the time we had finished it was early morning. We had talked all night. I felt more at peace with myself than I could ever remember. The anger and frustration that had been so prevalent in my life for many years was beginning to dissolve.

For the duration of the time she was there, we saw each other and dated regularly. Even though we became fast friends, and yes ultimately lovers, she continually encouraged me to go home and try to save my marriage. One might ask why she continued the relationship and risk heartbreak. Darlene later shared with me that she didn't expect to have serious feelings for me. As those feelings developed, she decided to encourage me to save my marriage because that was the right thing to do.

It was a big risk on her part because if I succeeded, I probably wouldn't see her again. But if my marriage didn't work out, she figured I would return to her. For her it was an acceptable risk. We agreed not to contact each other after she departed for her home duty station in Atlanta, GA. The relationship appeared to be over.

As I watched her drive away that Saturday morning, my heart broke. There was no way I could describe my feelings for her. I'd never felt this way about anyone before. I'd started out pursuing a conquest and had ended up with a friend, a confidant, and lover. Yes, I even found a soul mate. I began to wonder if I was experiencing real love for the first time in my life. Ironically, I had been searching for love all my life. And when I stopped searching, it seemed to have found me.

Well, you guessed it. I was the first to break our agreement. That night I called her to make sure she got home all right. Turns out that she wasn't upset that I called. She said she was about to call me. So, over the remainder of my temporary assignment, we talked daily. During one of our calls, there was a pause, and I quietly said, "I love you." There was silence, and then I heard her say, "I love you too."

Houston, we have a problem! Things were about to change, boy were they ever! Finally, my assignment was over, and I headed home knowing that there was about to be the mother of all fire storms, and I was not wrong.

I told my wife I wanted a divorce the day I got back. She was upset but not ballistic. However, two days later, she received a letter from one of my fellow instructors who had tried to date Darlene. She had refused him. The letter very specifically outlined dates, times, and places where Darlene and I had gotten together. You guessed it, the crap really hit the fan and the fight was on, a fight that would last for three years before the divorce would be final. To this day, Darlene and I still refer to those days as our "white-water days," referring to the condition of the water in Class Five Rapids. The good news, however, is that even white-water calms to a gentle flow as you move through it downstream.

For those of you out there who are either in or entering a white-water stage in your life, always remember, "This too shall pass." Later, I'll share how to make the best of those trying times and how to grow stronger in your relationship because of those struggles.

So, my personal life was in stressful crisis, and I was expending a lot of energy to fix it. At this point in my story, I feel I need to share some things with you. You may be experiencing a variety of feelings about this situation and about me as a person. Some of you are cheering me on, and some of you are loathing me as the lowest scum to ever draw breath. The truth is that you are both right to have those feelings for two reasons.

First, you are entitled to your personal feelings on all matters in life. Just be careful not to judge others based entirely on your feelings. I believe in the adage "you should never judge another until you have walked a mile in their moccasins." In addition, The Bible tells us that only God can judge or condemn the actions of another.

Second, life's daily events collectively play a huge role in our ultimate destination in life. Yes, the life I had lived for many years had turned me into a reprehensible person. But I still had a spark of good from my upbringing. Remember, there are times when good people do bad things, and there are times when bad people do good things.

I've learned that those are the times that prepare us to achieve the purpose that God has set out for us. It is during these times that we get glimpses of the unique talent that He has given us.

Don't forget the story of Saul, the Pharisee who had done a lot of evil. Yet, when God removed the scales from his eyes, he saw the truth and became Paul, one of Christ's Disciples. I'm not comparing myself to Paul or justifying my actions. I'm only pointing out how we all can change when God is in our lives. Please realize that God will still forgive you no matter how many horrible things you think you've done. The problem is often that we won't forgive ourselves and insist on holding on to the belief that we are not worthy and there is no chance of our redemption. Nothing is further from the truth if you're willing to make changes in your life and truly repent of your transgressions. Remember that God loves you and He resides within you as the emotion of love and positive energy. I say that not because I read it somewhere; no, I say it because I've felt it, I've lived it, and my life has changed because of it.

Okay, back to the story. Far be it from the army to keep drama out of my career while I tried to get my personal affairs in order. Nope, that would be too easy. I walked into my office one morning at about 7:30 a.m. and my phone was ringing. It was the battalion commander informing me that I had a call holding from Brigadier General John Connelly. I froze! My mouth went dry, and I became dizzy. First, generals don't call sergeants, and secondly, Brig. Gen. Connelly oversaw the massive investigation of recruiter malpractice in the early 1980's. Many NCOs' careers were ruined, and some even went to jail. In seconds, my entire time in recruiting flashed through my mind. Had I ever done anything illegal or inappropriate? Was my career about to be destroyed?

With more confidence than I was feeling, I lifted the receiver and said, "Good morning, Sir."

Without preamble he gruffly said, "How'd you like to go to Boston Sarge?"

"Well Sir, I'd really rather go to the Command Headquarters to the training section."

"Sarge, let me rephrase the question... how soon can you be in Boston?"

I immediately realized it was a rhetorical question. The decision had already been made. This was just one more seismic event in my already shaky life!

Chapter 4

So here I was in the middle of the perfect storm. My personal life was a disaster and the woman I loved was over 1000 miles away. On top of that, I was being sent to the Boston Recruiting Battalion by the general heading up a massive investigation of recruiters. What else could life throw at me? Oh, yea. My wife insisted on coming with me even though she was strongly fighting the divorce.

Even though my faith was nearly nonexistent, I still looked toward the heavens and said, "Lord I've heard that you'll never give us a load to carry greater than you give us the strength to carry it. But I think I've got all I can handle, so can you just knock it off for a while?"

My welcome to Boston was certainly anything but friendly. The storm continued. Everyone thought I was a plant from Brig. Gen. Connelly. During processing at the Brigade Headquarters, the Command Sergeant Major said, "I did everything I could to stop your assignment, and I don't want you here. I'll do everything in my power to screw up your career and get you reassigned."

My introduction to the Battalion Sergeant Major was no less threatening. He simply said, "I know a lot of people and my mission is to ruin you and your career, and I never fail a mission."

Welcome to Boston Recruiting Command. The Battalion Sergeant Major was a Special Forces Green Beret who had spent seven tours in Vietnam. I knew he meant what he said. As I walked out of the Sergeant Major's office, I was furious. These people aren't giving me a chance. All they want to do is ruin me. Well, they picked the wrong guy to mess with, I thought.

I reported to the recruiting station I would be commanding and met with the nine recruiters assigned to me. Now, the station I just took over had not achieved its monthly or annual mission (quota) for a very long time. I intended to change that. I held a meeting with all my recruiters and explained my plan. I assured them that I was not a plant with the intent of getting anyone fired. My mission, I told them, was to help them make their recruiting assignment a bright spot on their records. In the process, their improved performance would make the station successful. I explained that we had to be a tight-knit team and function as a single unit with a single mission and focus.

Within two months, we were making mission nearly every month, and the recruiters were receiving recognition for their efforts. I, however, was still getting nasty grams and nasty visits from the Battalion Sergeant Major. So much for success! I felt good about the success, but I was still living in the military quarters with my wife. In fact, our relationship had deteriorated into one long argument. My stress level was off the chart. What got me through those nights were my daily calls to Darlene and a 12-pack of beer. I was 39 at that time.

Then it happened. As I mentioned earlier, I was driving from Fort Devens, where I lived, to my recruiting station in Lowell, MA. It was 7 a.m. on the morning of March 15, 1981. Suddenly, I was overcome with enormous emotion. I began to sob and sweat; I had a horrible pain in my chest that made it hard to breathe. I couldn't drive. I had to pull off to the side of the road where I collapsed in the front seat of the car. All I wanted to do was die! There was nothing left for me; the stress of my family life and the threats from my superiors were more than I could take. It was over. I thought about how easy it would be to take my own life. I had lost all hope. But suddenly, I heard a voice in my head say, "Get help! Get help!"

At that instant, I thought of Darlene and how much I loved her. She was my reason to live. As I look back now, I know that God put that thought in my mind as His way of telling me that she and I were eternally connected. I believed that His mission for me included her as well. I'll tell you that has been proven to be true again and again over the past three plus decades. I will tell you that it was not religious doctrine that saved me that day. It was the Spirit of God; His love running through me. It is my belief that religion, while being very important to us, is each church's interpretation of God's word while spirituality is our direct connection to God through the emotion of love. There is a song by Tracy Byrd entitled, *"The Keeper of the Stars"*. It is a beautiful song about true love.

The words that Darlene and I believe apply to us are, *"Someone had a hand in it long before we ever knew; the keeper of the stars."* Find it and listen to it. It'll warm your heart.

Slowly I gained enough of my senses to be able to drive and I turned around and headed back to the base. My chest pain had subsided, and I didn't think I was having a heart attack. I felt it was more emotional and spiritual in nature, perhaps high anxiety. So, I went straight to the Catholic Chapel, since I'm Catholic I couldn't think of any other place to go. As I walked into the Chaplin's office, I began to calm down a little telling him I needed to talk to him right away. For the next forty-five minutes, I unloaded all the crap that was bothering me. When I finished, he just looked at me and said,

"Son your life is really screwed up. Unfortunately, it's such a mess, I'm not going to be able to help you."

I was devastated.

Then he said, "But I know who can." With that he reached for the phone.

It's amazing what can go through your mind when you are in a high state of anxiety and grief. My first thought was, are you kidding me, does he really have a direct line to The Man? He did not. He did, however, know someone at a stress center on base and that is where he sent me. The counselor I worked with was excellent. He took an approach that went straight to the heart of my issues. I'd like to share more about why he was able to do this, but unfortunately, I'm not sure how classified that information is. Suffice to say that he specialized in short term treatment of special operators returning from missions.

For the next year I saw him twice every week. In the beginning, he spent most of the time listening to me spill my guts about my life. After a few weeks, I felt much better and told him that I thought that I didn't need to come back anymore. That, I learned, was the wrong thing to say to him.

He looked at me with the eye of an angry drill sergeant and loudly said, "Sarge, look around the floor in this office and tell me what you see."

I looked around and saw nothing that stood out. So, I told him that all I could see was his carpet, a couple of throw rugs, and a wastebasket. With great frustration in his voice, he nearly screamed, "Don't you see all those little bags of crap laying all over the place that have strings that are tied to you? Those are the little balls of crap from your past. There are hundreds of them, and they are dragging you down. They are wearing you out and sapping your energy." Then came the order, "Sarge, you will not stop coming here twice a week until I tell you to stop, and that won't be until you've cleaned up all the crap you drag in here and mess up my office with. That's an order!"

That day he gave me a book to read before my next session. *"Why am I afraid to tell you who I am"*, by John Powell, a Jesuit Priest and theologian. It's a small book about 160 pages and easy to read. Over time, I read it so many times that it fell apart, and I had to get a new one. You owe it to yourself to get a copy and read it regardless of where you are in your life, whether you are experiencing difficulties or not. It will enrich your life.

So, over the next year I began to learn the importance of letting go of my past. I also learned to communicate more honestly without being afraid of the outcome. It was an enormous eye opener. During the year I was assigned to the Boston Recruiting Battalion, my time was divided between running the recruiting station, fighting to get a divorce, and learning how to live a more positive life. Of course, none of this would have ever been possible without Darlene's love and support. Fortunately, I was able to make several trips to Atlanta to see her.

In one of our sessions, my counselor explained to me that we all have what he called a reticular activating system, which consists of a small group of cells at the base of the brain. They act as a radar system constantly scanning for those things that support what we've set our mind on, such as goals and desires. He explained its operation like this: "You are driving down the interstate knowing you need to get off at a certain exit. But instead of looking for the exit, you begin to daydream. Suddenly, you snap out of the daydream when you realize that you are approaching your exit."

In essence, our minds operate automatically. He reiterated that our reticular activating system would bring our attention to anything that supports our goals and desires. Using that to my advantage, my counselor told me to write a letter to myself describing what my life would be like exactly five years from that day. He told me not to make it a narrative of what I'd like life to be like, but rather as a real time document.

Here is a part of what I wrote: "I awakened early and looked over at my beautiful wife Darlene, the light of my life. We feel more love for each other today than the day we married. We both have great jobs and are respected both professionally and as a couple. . ."

From that point forward, my reticular activating system went to work, and I began to recognize those things that would make that vision come true. As I look back, everything I put in that vision letter has come to pass, which proved to me the value of this exercise. Furthermore, it gave me direction at a time when I was totally confused. That direction would help me take advantage of opportunities that would come my way, which didn't take long to materialize.

It was my habit to get to the recruiting station early every morning to complete my paperwork and lay out plans for the day's activities. Shortly after my arrival, one of my NCOs would come in and make the coffee. One morning I was working away in my office when I became aware of a presence in the doorway. Without looking up, I said, "Sarge, don't just stand there. Get the coffee made." There was a short pause and a loud clearing of the throat. I looked up and realized that the presence in my doorway was Major General Maxwell Thurman, Commanding Officer of Army Recruiting Command.

To get the full impact of what I'd just done, you need to know a little about Mag. Gen. Thurman. He was a brilliant man. He knew what he wanted, and he delegated the right people to accomplish the task. God help you if you failed. The punishment could be brutal to your career.

I'd just called him Sarge and told him to make the coffee. I knew I was in big trouble. I jumped to my feet, greeted him properly and apologized for my mistake. To my surprise and great relief, he just said, "Sit down Sarge. I want to talk to you about your new assignment."

Two weeks later, I was in my new office at Army Recruiting Command Headquarters in Chicago. I was part of the effort to put a computerized sales system into every recruiting station in the United States. The purpose of the new system was to eliminate misrepresentation. The system included a 512K computer, a 17-inch television monitor and a digitalized disk showing all the various jobs and duty assignments that the Army had to offer. Also, there was a video on what to expect in basic training.

Yes, my chain of command in Boston stayed true to its word. Before I departed, the Battalion Sergeant Major called me into his office to officially tell me to get the hell out of his command. My evaluation report was a major train wreck. Now the maximum you can receive on your evaluation is 125. An evaluation of 120 hurts your career. But the score of 105 on my evaluation was devastating. Honestly, I was just glad to get out of there.

However, in the year I was there, we turned the station into a top producer and my recruiters were rewarded appropriately. Frankly that was all

I needed to be able to leave with a positive taste in my mouth.

The years I worked on the computerized recruiting project were a lot of fun and very special for me. First, we got Darlene reassigned to Army Recruiting Command so we could be together. At last, my divorce was finalized, and Darlene and I were married in 1983. This was my third marriage, and I was determined to do what it took to make it work. The best part was that we married not out of need but out of a deep love and a desire to serve each other.

My personal life was starting to get back on track and my professional life was looking better also. The bonus was that Darlene and I worked side by side on parts of the project, which was such a wonderful experience. We discovered that we naturally complemented each other and worked together as one. My level of confidence and self-worth were growing stronger every day. Darlene was a big part of that. Her support and encouragement gave me more confidence. That, in turn, helped me to play a critical role in the successful completion of the project.

At this point, some of you may be thinking that it must be great to have a spouse who can devote herself fully to supporting me without having issues of her own. Unfortunately, spouses have their own challenges they must deal with every day. Darlene was no different. In 1978 women in the Women's Army Corps were integrated into the regular Army. I can promise you that many women in the Army at that time have horror stories about their treatment. In short, my wife had her hands full with her own daily challenges. So how did we survive? It was simple but not always easy.

So here it is. First, we not only loved each other we liked each other as well. We were friends and I believe friendship is critical in any serious romantic relationship. Second, we recognized each other's challenges and agreed that neither one was more important than the other. Third, we openly communicated our upset and frustration with each other and worked together to address them.

Did we have disagreements and arguments? Certainly, but we learned how to disagree and argue without damaging our relationship or our love. I'll talk more about that later and share techniques on how to accomplish it. Finally, I want you to understand that I would not be where I am today if it were not for the love and support of my wonderful wife. We've been together 38 years, and we love each other more today than when we met. That love has been the foundation of our lives for many years, especially during our military careers. As I said before, that support made success possible at Recruiting Command, especially during the final phase of promoting the computer project to the Reagan Administration.

The Army first tested the system to ensure it would work and accomplish its purpose. My job was selling the concept to officers and to those who would approve funding for the system. Recruiting Command selected me as the primary person to conduct briefings where I would demonstrate the system to all levels of command and to some politicians. I was going back and forth from Chicago to Washington, D.C. so much that it felt more like I was assigned to the Pentagon rather than Fort Sheridan. Finally came the day to brief the U.S. Secretary of the Army. After all the work we had done, it came down to this one meeting. The decision would be made to approve it or reject it. Before I share what happened at the briefing, let me give you a little background on how the system worked so it'll make sense to you.

The recruiting process includes two commands, Recruiting Command, which interviews potential applicants, and the Military Enlistment Processing Station (MEPS), which conducts testing and physicals on potential enlistees. Our system was designed to show not only what potential enlistees could expect from the Army, but also what to expect at the MEPS. Since they are two separate commands, we had a separate piece of software for each. Remember, this was in the early 1980's and everything was on what was referred to as a floppy disc.

As we prepared to brief the Secretary of the Army, these two floppies were combined into one so that there was no need to switch software in the middle of the demonstration. The decision had been made that General Thurman and the colonel in charge of the project would conduct the briefing. I would only demonstrate the system if necessary. The briefing would be in Washington, D.C.

Before the briefing, I was nervous about sitting next to the Secretary of the Army. I had done many presentations on the system, but this was critical to the success of the project. Careers rode on this decision. The night before the briefing, I was preparing to leave for Washington, and Darlene sensed my nervousness. She sat me down and said, "You are very good at what you do. Don't worry because I know you are going to do very well." She hugged me and said, "You always respond very well to pressure. You know I love you and I will be right there with you in spirit."

Early the next morning, I was working with the IT professional setting up the equipment, getting ready in case a demonstration became necessary. Unfortunately, he had laid the floppy disc on the table next to the computer system, not realizing that I had set my coffee close by. In the process of setting up the system, I bumped my cup and spilled coffee on the floppy disk ruining it. This could be a disaster! I asked him to get the backup disc. He said he didn't bring one. My heart sank. I then asked him if he'd brought copies of the two original discs, and he said he hadn't. Oh my God, what do we do now? We were less than 45 minutes from the briefing. I dug around in the bottom of my briefcase and found badly beat up copies of the original two discs. In fact, we were not sure they would work. But they were all we had. We crossed our fingers.

I put the first one in the system and slowly it booted up. It was usable. I started to switch discs, and the IT professional stopped me saying that the disc might not boot again so I should leave it up. That meant that I had no idea if the second one would work and wouldn't find out until I was in front of the Secretary. Please God don't make me do a demonstration, I was thinking.

The briefing began and the General and the Colonel did a great job of explaining the system and the test results. When they were finished, the Secretary said, "It all looks great, but I can never sell the President on this because he thinks all defense dollars should go to boots and bullets and not computer projects. I'm sorry."

With that Gen. Thurman stepped up and said, "Mr. Secretary before you go, I'd like to have Sgt.

Nicholas demonstrate the system for you so you can see it in operation."

I froze. Oh my God, I'm going to have to do this, I thought. What if it doesn't work? Scratch one military career. I'm toast. The pressure was enormous. I thought this must be what a field goal kicker feels like when he is called on to win the Super Bowl with one second on the clock, attempting the longest kick of his career. If he misses, he lets everyone down, the team, the fans, and his family. No doubt, he would be remembered as the guy who choked at the most important time in his career.

It was then that I thought of what Darlene had said the night before about my ability to perform under pressure. Her confidence assured me that I wasn't going to choke. My thoughts went from negative to positive. Like the kicker, I was ecstatic to have the game in my hands. When it's all on the line I want the ball in my hands. My eyes met Gen. Thurman's, and I knew that he believed in me. It was time to get on with the game.

The Secretary and I sat at the computer, and I started the demonstration. When I finished the recruiting station portion of the demonstration, I pulled the disc out and put in the second disc. You could have heard a pin drop. It felt like all the air had been sucked from the room. There were no less than 15 high-level officers and civilians wondering what I was doing. They had been told that the full presentation was on one disc.

Since the beginning of the demonstration, a hand had been resting on my shoulder. I was so focused on my job that I never turned around to see who it was. Now the hand squeezed harder, and I could see the Secretary becoming uncomfortable. There was a pause as the computer attempted to boot. The silence was deafening to the point where I felt I needed to create a distraction while it booted. Then it hit me.

"Mr. Secretary, in all my previous briefings I've been asked if recruiters would be afraid to use the system for fear of messing it up since computers are so new. The answer to that question is 'no'. In fact, they're told that they can't hurt the system."

With that I started pounding on the keyboard and it was beeping and beeping. I then looked at him and said, "If however, you pound on it too hard, a long hairy arm will reach out from the computer and grab you by the throat." Oh God, I thought, where did that come from? This is the Secretary of the Army crying out loud. You don't make smart ass remarks to people like him. No doubt my career is really toast now, I thought. The Secretary looked at me and smiled, seemingly amused at my comment.

At that moment, the computer decided to fully boot up and I was able to complete the demonstration. Shortly afterward, I began the second part of the demonstration, and the hand that had been on my shoulder since the beginning of the demonstration went away. Thank God it's over, I thought. I just need to get out of here. But as I finished, the Secretary slid back from the table and said, "Okay gentlemen you've got yourself a system. You'll have your funding within the next month." He then turned to me and said, "Thank you Sergeant for the demonstration and be careful that the hairy arm doesn't come out and get you." He smiled, shook my hand and left.

I was shaking all over. People were hugging me and cheering. I know that's unusual for this type of military meeting. But there had been so much on the line. As I moved away from the computer, I closed my eyes and said, "Thank you God and thank you for my wonderful wife."

As we were leaving the briefing room, the Colonel stopped me and asked, "Do you know whose hand was on your shoulder?"

I said, "No I don't."

He said, "It was General Thurman, and as he took his hand from your shoulder, he leaned over to me and said, 'You don't need me here anymore. We just got ourselves a system.'"

Chapter 5

One of the happiest days of my life was the day I married Darlene on July 30, 1983. We had been together for three years before my divorce was finalized. In December of 1984 we were re-assigned to Atlanta.

The move from Chicago to our new assignments in Atlanta was a giant step in my journey back to God. Over the next 4 years, what we learned brought us to where we are today and the discovery of God's purpose for both of us.

It was during this time that I worked with a Christian Counselor, who I will refer to as Coach. It had been three years since my last counseling session in Boston. I returned to counseling because I knew that there was so much more that I could learn to make life better. Moreover, I realized that I still had some issues with trust and anger.

From Coach and through personal experience, I learned that our lives are directed by the decisions we make, and those decisions are made based on our feelings at the time. There are hundreds of feelings, but there are only two emotions: **love and fear**. I learned that decisions made from the emotion of fear normally bring negative results because fear is a negative energy. Those decisions made from love are normally very positive because love is a positive energy. That energy comes from God because He is love. To be able to make the most of your decisions from the emotion of love, it is necessary to learn how to master fear. In fact, almost every day we must decide whether we are going to control fear or allow fear to control us. That decision is critical because it determines who is guiding our lives, God or Satan.

It is my opinion that fear represents Satan. This opinion does not come from formal research or academic exposure, but from having lived through it with God's help and my counselors' guidance. I will talk more about this later.

Once I realized that everything in our lives is controlled by either fear or love, it completely changed the way I looked at life. Most importantly, I grasped the understanding that Satan was controlling me when I allowed fear to determine my direction. Even more importantly, I understood that God was directing my life when I was controlled by love.

Even though I would reason that I wasn't afraid, negative feelings would override my reason. Then I would use reason to deny my feelings and suppress my fear, a vicious cycle. My coach taught me that understanding my feelings were a key to controlling fear.

We connect with everything in our lives with feelings and those feelings are attached to emotions, either fear or love. Let's qualify love. We most often think of love in the romantic sense. But I am referring to love as positive energy, which moves us in a positive direction. In contrast, fear is negative energy and moves us in a negative direction.

Knowing this didn't change life's adversities. The daily challenges kept right on coming. But it did change how I responded to those challenges. Before this revelation, I never would have looked at challenges as positive situations or events. In my view, they would have been just one more way of making my life more difficult and more miserable. I honestly believe that most people reading this book feel the same way.

I believe the mindset that most of us have is, "If I can overcome this next challenge everything will be okay. Life will be perfect." The truth is that each challenge is just one more obstacle on the journey of life. I now understood that it's not how big or small the challenge is. Rather, it's how we perceive the challenges and respond to them. In situations where the event is tragic, it would be impossible to define that event as positive. The question is do we respond with positive or negative energy? There is no question that our first response will be filled with negative feelings such as anger, confusion, sorrow, and grief. After the initial shock, it becomes necessary for us to make a myriad of decisions regarding the tragedy.

One of the most important is "how am I going to let this situation affect my life?" This decision is extremely important. We can either make it based on our negative feelings, which can lead to anger and bitterness. Or we can look at it through positive feelings, which can move us toward hope for the future. It is important to realize that there are two sides to every coin, a positive outcome and a negative outcome. We often cannot change the event. But we can choose how we allow it to affect us.

For example, the three tragic events of my youth, my mother's death, my high school sweetheart's betrayal, and my first wife's cheating shocked my senses at first. Unfortunately, after the initial shock wore off, I made a major mistake. Instead of making decisions about my future based on positive feelings, I chose to continue being bitter, angry, and vengeful. So, for many years, I blocked my opportunities for happiness and a bright future. I wallowed in my own misery using alcohol and womanizing to cope with my emotional pain. I always blamed others for my misery, thus giving away control of my life.

Darlene and I were now married and living in Atlanta. We believed that we were past the white water. Life was running smoother, and we'd had some exciting things happen in our lives. So now we live happily ever after, right? Wrong! To us it appeared that life just kept throwing crap in the game. Why? We're doing our best to do what's right and good. But we keep running into all these major challenges. Why were our lives so full of problems while others seemed to be living a good life? Many would ask, "Are we being punished for past sins?"

I thought that God was supposed to forgive us and never give us a heavier load to carry than the strength we must carry it. Those thoughts alone would be enough to make you question if there really is a God. However, I had learned that those challenges were not there as punishment from God, but as a way of making us stronger so that we could carry out the mission he had set out for us. In addition, each of those challenges provided an opportunity for us to learn more about how to handle life's daily onslaught. Even though I didn't believe that He was punishing us, we still felt the pain of those situations. Here is the truth; working through the pain made us stronger. It was at times very difficult but necessary.

For example, my transfer from Chicago to Atlanta was smooth. However, Darlene and I wanted to be assigned together. But her transfer was a major challenge requiring the intervention of Gen. Thurman. If you are familiar with the military, you know that any time a General gets involved, it has wide ranging consequences. For Darlene it created a career crisis.

It turned out that her senior NCO was from the old school and had little or no respect for females in the Army. The first strike against her was that Gen. Thurman had been involved in her assignment. Second strike was that she was a very good NCO and very good at her job. The third strike was that she was a reservist on a long-term activity duty tour. Unlike today, many of the old-school soldiers looked at reservists in the same vein as they did draft dodgers. It was thought that all of them had joined the reserves and National Guard to avoid being drafted. It made no difference to her senior NCO that she had volunteered for active duty earlier in her career.

It turns out that her boss excelled at psychological warfare. He placed her desk in a position where he could stare at her while she worked. Then he would walk behind her and look over her shoulder at her work, often making disparaging remarks. He never openly criticized her. He did it with stealth so that it was his word against hers. He belittled her every way he could until he destroyed her self-confidence.

Imagine being singled out by your boss and being harassed every day. Yes, in today's workplace that would be strong grounds for a formal complaint to human resources. Not so in the Army at that time. She spoke with those above her in the chain of command with little or no relief. Again, it was during the time of the continued integration of the women into the regular army and she was dealing with male NCOs and officers.

She became more and more depressed as the months went by. Her confidence and her emotional well-being were being destroyed. Of course, as her husband, I wanted to jump in and make the problem go away. Based on my infantry background, I wanted to have a private conversation with the individual and explain to him the error of his ways. That, however, probably would have been a bad idea.

Darlene became very upset with me for trying to interfere. She explained to me that she was a NCO and she would handle the situation as a NCO. She said that she was responsible for taking care of the situation.

However, the situation was exacerbated by two factors. First, I was thinking like a husband whose wife was being mistreated. At the same time, I was experiencing old feelings of jealousy and mistrust from my past. All the ingredients were there for our relationship to experience a major explosion.

So how did we handle it? At this point I was working with Coach, and, with his guidance, we worked through. He taught us the importance of open and honest communication and total openness in expressing our feelings and emotions to each other without personal attacks.

The first thing we learned to do was to lay all the cards on the table and come to agreement that all situations were important. Secondly, he taught us to argue and even fight without damaging our relationship. The key, he explained, was that we express our points of view openly. It was critical that we stay focused on the action and not the person. Never attack the other personally. Instead, always attack the action. Let me use a simple but humorous example.

When Darlene and I first got married, I had a bad habit of leaving the lid up on the toilet. Finally, one morning she'd sat on the cold porcelain one too many times. She got right up in my face and said, "I love you with all my heart, but I will no longer tolerate you leaving the lid up on the toilet. It makes me very angry, so stop it." The way she handled it was perfect. Most would have handled it differently and said something like, "How many times have I told you to put the lid down? I can't believe you are so stupid and thoughtless that you would continue to ignore my request. If you loved me, you wouldn't be so uncaring."

As you can see in the second scenario, she would have been attacking me personally, accusing me of being stupid and uncaring. Most of us push back when attacked and the situation escalates. So, to avoid the personal attacks so common in many relationships, we sat down and set some ground rules for handling conflicts between us.

Here are those rules:

1. When we recognize a conflict or a time when there is something bothering us, we simply say, *"I feel like I'm walking on eggshells, and we need to clear the air."* If it is a situation that has a lot of raw emotion attached to it, we simply say, *"Before we sit down, I need a little space to fully understand my feelings."* Then we spend time alone clarifying the issue before we talk about it.

2. When we sit down to discuss the issues, the first step is to put every issue on the table and agree that all are equally important. A caveat to this is that if one of the issues has an immediate negative consequence or is time sensitive, we handle that one first.

3. As we discuss the issues, we will honestly and openly express our thoughts and feelings without reservation and without fear of retribution. We listen to each other with an open and receptive mindset.

4. Once all thoughts and feelings are out in the open, we will each give input regarding various solutions for the situation. Then we select the one that provides the best outcome for the situation and for our relationship. It is important that we keep our love and friendship

for each other at the forefront of all discussions throughout the process.
5. We hold each other, reaffirm our love for each other, and pray for God's guidance.

I would love to tell you that there is always a perfect solution for each situation. However, in real life sometimes you must do the best you can with the cards you are dealt, never forgetting that every hand is a winner, and every hand is a loser. The difference is determined by whether your decisions are made from positive or negative thoughts.

In Darlene's case, after two years of constant stress from dealing with disrespect and personal harassment, she was diagnosed with a serious stress-driven disease causing physical and emotional pain. In fact, she resigned from active duty and transferred to the Individual Ready Reserve. Soon after she left active duty, she took a position with Hewlett Packard as executive assistant to the Southeast Regional Sales Manager. This turned out to be another of God's blessings because the experience she gained became invaluable when we started our own business after I retired from the Army.

As difficult as it was, I allowed Darlene to handle her own situation. I stayed out of it giving her the time and space to vent whenever she felt the need to do so. Sometimes she would ask me my opinion about some aspect of the situation. But I never stepped in and told her what to do, nor did I try to take control of the situation. Ultimately, no matter how it turned out, she knew I was there for her as her best friend. As her husband, I loved her unconditionally.

Liking each other and being friends has been critical to our successful marriage.

Not long ago I was coaching a couple who had been living together for several years and finally decided to get married. As in all my coaching with couples, I asked them two important questions. First, do you love each other? Their response was overwhelmingly yes, and they spent several minutes extoling the virtues of their love. Secondly, I asked do you like each other? The ensuing silence was deafening. Finally, they started saying things like, some of the time, not always, and not when he or she does this or that.

Liking your partner is important because to like is a positive feeling generated by the positive energy of love. Arguments and disagreements occur throughout our relationships. However, if you like someone you are far less inclined to try to attack and destroy that person. In my opinion, strong, long-lasting relationships are built on a foundation of friendship wrapped in the emotion of love.

When I am working with people who are having problems in relationships, I have them focus on what they like or don't like about each other instead of whether they love each other. They are two different conversations. Love will wax and wane, but liking a person is the foundation of the relationship. Then I get them to have open conversations about what they don't like, why they don't like it, and why the other person feels they have those traits.

Often, they can work through these issues and find they like their partners more than they realized. Sometimes, though, we must agree to disagree because we don't live in a perfect world. I believe that most of us have met people we didn't like from the minute we met them. But over time, as we came to know them better, we understood them and became friends.

When Darlene and I are asked what we consider the secret to our many happy years of marriage, we tell them we like each other, and we were friends before we were lovers. You see, for a long time after that night I tried to seduce her, I tried to figure out why I didn't just tell her to leave, and why was I so willing to unload all those secrets of my life onto a near stranger. It is because I liked her. I liked who she was. I liked her strength of character and how she stood by her decisions.

We have had our table discussions many times. During those times, we have learned to strengthen our ability to communicate at a deeper level.

With Coach's help, we learned that there are three levels of response in communication:

1. **Our automatic response -** Instead of being open and vulnerable to answering questions, we give each other programmed responses. We follow the safest path, giving programmed responses to open-ended questions rather than revealing what we think and how we feel. It is the same as saying, *"I don't feel comfortable sharing my thoughts and feelings."* Fortunately, I had a colleague who shared with me a wonderful phrase he would use to move a conversation from the auto response to the thinking response in a non-threating manner. *"I find that interesting. Can you share a little more about that?"* This leaves the other person feeling more in control of the conversation. He can share a little or a lot, but he is now more engaged in the conversation focusing on the issue. Of course, to share more information, it is necessary to think about what you want to say.

2. **Our thinking level** – Once the person reaches the thinking level, he or she will begin to share more of his or her thoughts. This is important because what people think also reveals the logic which they are using to justify their decisions about how to handle the issues. The

key here is to get both parties' thoughts and feelings on the table so that the discussion can be honest and open.

3. **Our feeling level** – To get to the feeling level, we learn to use this type of phrase: *"I find your thoughts on the issue to be interesting and enlightening. If you would, please share with me how you feel about these insights."* Again, this is important because we have now revealed the other person's thoughts and feelings on the issue. We should now be able to discuss it and come to a decision on how to handle the issue that is acceptable to both parties in most cases. Another question that can help is: *"Share with me if you will why do you feel that way?"* This question, however, can be intrusive. The point is to allow the other person to feel in control, which gives him or her confidence to have an open discussion.

The key to this entire process is the use of questions. There is magic in asking questions. You see, when I ask you a question you take ownership of the answer, as you should; however, you also automatically take ownership of the question as well. The magic is that now the whole idea becomes yours not mine.

There are times when people are not fully honest in their responses. This can be because they are fearful that honest answers will be too revealing, making them more vulnerable. However, using this questioning method provides them with a greater level of comfort allowing them to be more relaxed in the conversation. Having learned this process, Darlene and I have found that it has enabled us to not only communicate better with each other but to also communicate better with those around us.

Learning this process was critical in strengthening the foundation of our relationship both then and now. Even though we love each other and like each other, the issues from our past occasionally continue to challenge our relationship today. As in every relationship, each person brings their own baggage to it. For the relationship to remain strong, it is necessary for both parties to put the issues on the table and come to a consensus decision on how to deal with them. Failure to address these issues in the long run will damage or destroy the relationship.

For example, I had some major trust issues because of past experiences with women who had betrayed me and had broken my heart. Even though the counseling I'd gotten while I was in Boston had helped me to get them under control, they still surfaced from time to time. They caused quite a bit of tension early in our relationship. At times I would become sullen, unresponsive, and downright argumentative with Darlene over some innocent interaction she had with another man.

Darlene has an outgoing nature and has male and female friends. Obviously, those interactions triggered my issues of distrust and jealousy. Unfortunately, I would hold these thoughts and feelings inside and let them fester. Darlene, on the other hand, couldn't understand why I was acting the way I was because she had never thought once about betraying me.

When she would ask me what was wrong, I would say "nothing," which is an *auto-response*. But my body language told a different story.

Then she would say, "Something is bothering you. Share it with me."

One day she did something that upset me, and I just looked at her and said, "What you just did really pissed me off!" I was shocked when she broke out laughing hysterically.

"Finally," she said, "you expressed your feelings. Why haven't you done this before?"

I immediately shot back, "I was afraid to because I might make you mad, and you'd leave me like all of the other women in my life." This was a big breakthrough. But we knew that I still had a lot of work to do.

At my next meeting with Coach, I shared what had happened. Instead of telling me what to do he, as usual, asked me a question. "Why do you think you finally opened up like that?" he asked.

I thought for a minute and said, "I guess it was because the pain I felt holding it in was greater than the fear of what would happen if I spoke out." He asked me to think about it and suggested that Darlene and I discuss it.

Darlene and I knew that repressing my feelings was bad and unhealthy. So, she agreed to look for signs that I was holding back my feelings and then tell me that she sensed I was struggling with something. This was important because I'd become so accustomed to holding in my feelings that I was seldom aware that I was doing it. To make it easier and less threatening we agreed on a "safe phrase." When she suspected that I was having a problem, she'd simply say, "I think I see turkey. Can we talk about it?"

Turkey referred to the negative thoughts and feelings I was having at any given time since she would often recognize them before I would.

In the process, I did not ask her to change her behavior. That was important because asking her to be someone she wasn't to satisfy my issues would have ultimately destroyed us. I had to let her be herself and she had to let me be myself. We can be individuals within our marriage relationship. Yet, we are one as a couple. Many people get married with the belief that they can change their spouses after they are married. Unfortunately, it seldom ever works and often has a disastrous ending.

Chapter 6

During my lifetime, I had hit bottom. However, fortunately, I received enough help to change my way of thinking, which changed my life. Up until the point I met Darlene, fear controlled my life in the form of negative thoughts and feelings. Before I met her, I felt that life had slammed its door in my face, and I felt that nothing positive was going to happen again. I made up my mind I would not live one day beyond the age that mother had; she died at 52. I had given up on life and felt like a dead man walking. I was only waiting for the body to give out because everything else had already died.

After I met Darlene, I began to see a small bright light of hope because of all the loving support she was providing. It had taken me 38 years to arrive at that point in my life. After experiencing the joy of the positive side of life, I had a deep desire to make the necessary changes to maintain that lifestyle.

The problem was that, like most people, I wanted to change immediately. But after talking with Coach, and having conversations with Darlene, I came to understand that this was not going to be a sprint. Rather, I realized that it was going to be a journey, and I was not sure of the outcome.

Since we don't see the future, we don't fully see the impact of changes on our lives at the time. I realized that life must be lived one day at a time. My job was to focus more on the positive each day and less on the negative. Each day I was one step closer to achieving the true happiness that I felt was now possible. But could I let go of the past long enough to enjoy the present?

We all tend to allow the past to have too much influence on us. The past is past. Let go of the past. You can't change it. You can't fix it. It is just there. We are afraid that there is something we should have learned and didn't. Unfortunately, we don't understand that anything we fail to learn will come around again and give us another chance to learn it. We should not be afraid of this, however, because it will come back in a different context. But it will be different because we will have learned more since the last go around, and we will be able to make the necessary changes to improve the situation. It has been said that "when the student is ready the teacher will appear."

What I learned to do was to look forward to the future knowing that many great things awaited me. The future was bright. But I also learned that the future wasn't here yet. So, I shouldn't live in the future either. There was only one place left to live: fully in the present. Tomorrow is determined by today's actions. That convinced me to live in the present. The most exciting thing I learned was that I had the power to determine my own future. But when we allow fear to control our lives, we place dark shadows over our future. I know this for a fact because I have been there.

So many negative things had happened to me in the past, which had challenged my trust. Therefore, I couldn't bring myself to believe that there was any possibility of a good relationship in my future. Anything positive that indicated that I had a bright future was outside of my self-image and certainly outside of my comfort zone.

What I mean by dark shadows is all those negative events in our past that we still carry with us today. Like it or not they still impact the decisions we make. Therefore, they are close at hand and play a part in shaping our self-image. Since they affect our self-image, they also affect how we view our future. That's what Coach and I went to work on.

Chapter 7

It would take time to make changes. Coach deserves a great deal of credit for my progress. Through our interactions and real-life experience, I learned *that long-term change would not occur until the pain of the present became greater than the fear of the change.* It is critical to understand that progress is three steps forward and two steps back.

My lack of trusting women, for example, was one of my major issues. Working with Coach, I was learning to strengthen my trust in Darlene. Honestly, I was making good progress. However, what I learned was that this new trust was completely outside of what had been my belief for nearly 40 years. As a result, I would pull back from the trust and look for any action she would take that would support my old way of acting. Basically, we were re-programming my computer to accept a different program. But my brain, the computer, would at times reject the new way of behaving.

Darlene has a very friendly, outgoing personality. She likes people. I would see her talking with another man, being friendly, and I would fall back into my old way of thinking. That night I would accuse her of flirting with other men, a product of dark shadows. And from there the argument would ensue. Thank God we had learned to argue without damaging our relationship. On my next visit to Coach, I'd say, "I thought I was doing so well. So why does this keep coming up? I know better but I can't seem to help myself."

He would simply say, "Remember that you're on a journey. You're learning to drastically change how you live your life. As I told you in the past, change is three steps forward and two steps back."

He went on to explain, "You do not control her. She is going to make her own decisions. If she decides to cheat, she is responsible for that choice. You will feel devastated. But you need to realize that the devastation comes from your fear of humiliation, fear of inadequacy, and all those negative feelings you have experienced in other parts of your life. So, understand that even if she did (cheat), you are going to be alright because you are going to find a way to handle your situation." Coach told me many times that I possessed the knowledge and ability to handle the situation. It may not be pleasant, but it won't be the end of the world.

As I mentioned before, there is an adage that when the student is ready the teacher will appear. I believe that. All the things that had happened up to that point had prepared me to hear and learn what I needed to know to achieve greater personal growth and more peace of mind. Now I was ready for breakthroughs in my way of thinking.

In our first two meetings, I told Coach all the things that had happened to me in my life. His responses were simply to ask me what I thought or felt about those events. Then in our next session, he asked me a lot of questions about several of the events. After listening carefully to my responses, he shared with me his view on my situation. He told me that, like many other people, I often felt confused about what was happening in my life. My feelings, he said, caused me to experience uncertainty in my current situation. Moreover, those negative feelings were blocking my ability to see the bigger picture and make the proper decisions necessary to move in a positive direction.

Coach explained to me that my emotional turmoil was destroying my self-confidence and negatively impacting my self-esteem. Therefore, since I saw myself as unworthy, I was making decisions that would support how I felt about myself. I asked why I would do such a silly thing because I thought I was making decisions to get myself out of my situation.

He smiled and explained that we all have an image of ourselves. As a result, we develop a comfort zone that accepts thoughts and actions that support that image, negative as it might be. If we do things or take actions outside of that comfort zone, which make us feel better, we begin to realize that this new feeling does not match our self-image. Strange as this might sound, our old undeserving self-image is known and comfortable to us. Therefore, we become frightened of the positive change and jump back into the old behavior so we're back in our comfort zone.

The downside to this type of this behavior is that we return to the same old actions that caused our problem. The upside, Coach explained, is that every time we go outside of our comfort zone, the zone itself stretches and it never goes back to the way it was one hundred percent. So, the more times we go out of our comfort zone the bigger it gets. The process of spiritual growth, therefore, is a three-step forward, two-step back proposition. That is not what I wanted to hear. But at least I could see that I was making progress dealing with my negative feelings rooted in the past.

Coach continued, "Unfortunately, most people who seek major change in their lives don't find it because they abandon the process after the first or second time they have a setback. They simply say, "well that didn't work" and quit."

He concluded that all the negative things that had happened in my life had put me in constant emotional turmoil, causing me to lose a lot of control of my life. The good things, like Darlene, had provided me with some sense of stability to keep me from losing all my control.

He said, "In fact, Darlene is your rock. You can count on the fact that she loves you, supports you and totally believes in you. Unfortunately, because of your self-image, you are doing things to sabotage her efforts because you won't allow yourself to accept that you are deserving of her love and support. If you want to achieve a happier and more peaceful life, you're going to need to *reclaim your life*."

So, I told Coach that I thought what he said made sense, but that I didn't know what to do to make the necessary changes. I asked him if he could give some ideas on how I could make those changes, which he did. Over the next several visits, he began to explain concepts that I'd never thought about. As a result, I could more fully understand how I got to where I was and how I could change my self-image and reclaim my life.

One of the first concepts he shared was difficult for me to get my head around, I guess, because I'd never heard it before. He told me that our lives are sustained by our ability to breathe, but our direction in life is determined by the decisions we make.

He said, "You are exactly where you are because of the decisions you've made your whole life." Then he really got my attention when he said, "Every decision I'd ever made was based on how I felt at the time." More shockingly, he said, "Each one of those decisions was tied to an emotion." In short, he told me that my life was directed by my emotions and because of my emotional turmoil I had brought myself to this place in life.

Coach told me more than once that there are hundreds of feelings but only two emotions. I have said this before and it is worth repeating: The two emotions are love, which is positive, and fear, which is negative. Everything else is a feeling derived from one of those two emotions. He went on to explain that fear spawns negative feelings such as hate, anger, and jealousy. Love spawns positive feelings such as compassion, caring, and forgiveness.

Then he asked me a simple question, "Have you ever felt hate for anyone and why?" I was floored that he would ask that question after all I'd told him about my life.

So, I said, "That's a silly question. You can pick any of the people in my past who have screwed me over."

He told me to give him an example. "Okay," I said, "I was bullied badly in school. The guy who bullied me was much bigger than me and was constantly doing things to physically harm me. In fact, one time he tied my hands behind my back and rolled me up in a wrestling mat so tightly that I passed out from lack of air. Thank God a teacher heard me scream and got me out. So, yes, I had the emotion of hate for him."

Coach corrected me. He said, "Hate is a feeling not an emotion. So, what were you afraid of that caused you to feel hatred for him?"

I thought for a minute and said, "I feared him because he took away all my control. He physically abused me and at one point nearly killed me."

"Exactly," Coach said, "but in fact it wasn't the bully you feared. Rather, it was the loss of control that caused the feeling and directly impacted how you made your decisions. Unfortunately, your mind recorded the event complete with a full-color video and an emotional soundtrack that, when triggered, would play and you'd relive the event in in your mind. Therefore, every time you felt threatened in any way, the tape would play, and you'd react to the threat with a fear-based decision."

He explained, "Our brain, like a computer, records every event in our lives, positive and negative. Those experiences can be pulled up at any moment because of some trigger like a song or a movie, or just some mention of a past event relating to the situation. Immediately you relive the event and decide based on the feelings and emotion generated by the event. Therefore, because of the constant emotional turmoil you experienced, you spend a lot of time making decisions based on the negative events from your past. Now here is where it is critical that you understand the power of emotions in taking control of your life.

"Our decisions are made based on our feelings, and all our feelings are based on either the emotion of love or fear. That means positive or negative energy directs our lives. Unfortunately, until you stop feeling hatred for the bully, he will always have an impact on how you respond to any perceived threat. In other words, he will always be controlling some part of your life. Now, if you take that same approach in dealing with betrayal by those whom you believed in – especially the women in your life – you will react based on those feelings of distrust and make decisions based on negative feelings. The result will be that you find it difficult trust anyone, and, even if you do, you will always be looking for the slightest indication of any unfaithfulness or deception on their part, wondering when the next shoe is going to drop. Just like the bully, as long your decisions are impacted in this way, those people will maintain a level of control of your life."

Then he asked me if I was beginning to see how I was giving control of my life to a lot of different people. He said that at this point in my life I'd given a vast portion of control of my life to others. Sadly, I realized they didn't know they had that control and frankly probably didn't give a damn anyway. I said, "Sounds great Coach, but how in the world do I get back that control?"

His response provided me with one of the many great insights that helped me to learn the things I needed to learn to continue my journey, achieving the deep peace I feel today.

He smiled at me and said, "I'm going to teach you how to manage your fear and change your approach to making decisions so that you can take back control of your life." He went on to explain that learning to manage my fear and changing the way I made my decisions would enable me to achieve more positive results. Consequently, I would be able to achieve the personal and professional goals I sought. That made perfect sense to me. Unfortunately, it was going to take some time and effort to make these changes and become more proficient at making my decisions.

He said, "Nick, let me start by asking you to tell me what fear is in your words."

"Well," I replied, "I guess it's what people feel when they are frightened or scared of something that's happening to them."

"That's true," he said. "It's also an emotion as I said earlier. Unfortunately, however, neither of those are definitions that we can use to successfully handle challenges in our lives because we don't always recognize fear as the problem. Instead, we react to the feeling that the situation generates. For example, assume your boss yells at you or gives you a poor performance rating. You are most likely going to experience anger or frustration. But it is unlikely that you will associate that feeling with *fear*. That means you will react to your feelings rather than the emotion of fear. As a result, you end up addressing the symptom (feeling) rather than addressing the problem (the emotion of fear).

"Therefore, I'm going to give you a working definition of fear that you can use to change how you make your decisions, making it possible to find the peace you are seeking. It's important for you to understand that where you are in life at this very moment is based on the decisions you've made. Again, it's important that I remind you that you've never made a good or bad decision. You've only made decisions. If they gave you the result you wanted, you labeled it a good decision. On the other hand, if they didn't give you what you wanted, you labeled them bad and probably beat yourself up for making bad decisions.

"So, here is a working definition of fear. Fear is a question. Am I going to be okay? Think about any time you have felt fear. The first question you asked, conscious or otherwise, was '*Am I going to be okay? Am I going to survive this*?' Most of the time we answer the question with a resounding '*I don't know,*' which only exacerbates the level of our fear.

"Here is the answer to the question that will give you control of your fears. *'Yes, I'm going to be okay because God gave me the skills, knowledge and ability to handle anything that comes my way.'*

"Think about it. You've endured everything that's happened to you in life up to now and survived it. The reason is that regardless of your situation, you have been able to use your skills, knowledge and ability to handle the situation. You may not have got the outcome you wanted, but you handled it, you survived, and you're still standing."

He continued. "In the years since I learned this definition and shared it with others, I've been challenged by those who ask me, *'what if it kills me?'* My response is that death is a part of life. I promise you that you will use all your skill, knowledge, and abilities to prevent death. If it still occurs, then it was God's will, and nothing could have stopped it."

When Coach finished explaining the concept, I had to question him before I could get my head around it. I told him that I didn't think that I felt a significant presence of fear when making decisions. He immediately corrected me saying that I had made decisions based on feelings that were attached to the emotion of fear.

"There are hundreds of feelings, but there are only two emotions," he said. "All feelings are generated by one emotion or the other, love or fear."

Here is what Coach taught me. I will use an example that everyone will be able to relate to. Have you ever gotten up in the morning dressed for work and then felt uncomfortable about what you were wearing? You could have felt uncomfortable for several reasons. Will people think I look funny? Will I fit in with the others? Is what I'm wearing out of style?

These are all negative feelings attached to the emotion of fear. Our normal response in this situation is to second guess ourselves and choose different attire. When we give in to the negative feelings and second-guess our decision, we, unfortunately, lose some of our self-confidence and esteem. In the process, we give control to people who don't really care one way or the other.

Once you learn to recognize that you are second-guessing yourself because of a negative feeling, you can reevaluate the issue more carefully and then decide based on the actual information you have available at the time, rather than solely on concern over what others might or might not think. This is the difference between responding and reacting to a situation.

"Let me clarify what I mean by giving control to others," Coach said. "Our lives are controlled by the decisions we make every day, some conscious some unconscious. As I have said, those decisions are made based on feelings attached to emotion. Therefore, when we allow negative feelings about the opinions of others to determine our decision, they have control over the direction of our lives. Do not misunderstand me. This does not mean that we should disregard the thoughts and opinions of others or of society. Listen to them, evaluate them and learn from them when appropriate, but don't be afraid to live your life based on your own personal values and ethics."

Over the next several sessions we went into more detail about how our lives are directed by our decisions and how we make those decisions. At one point, he shared with me how our decisions are influenced by previous events in our lives. He chuckled when he said this, "People go to psychologists to solve present day problems, and it seems that the only thing the psychologist wants to talk about is their past."

Naturally, Coach explained, when a current event triggers a previous event, the tape of the previous event plays in our mind as if it were happening right now. Because of this, the feelings we experience are exactly or very similar to the feelings we experienced in the past. Unfortunately, we are not necessarily aware that the decision we are about to make today is associated with an event that may have happened many years ago. *Moreover, the feelings from the past event may cause us to override or ignore our higher level of knowledge or different facts now available to us.* Often, we don't even recognize the trigger to the event as the trigger. So, we can end up making the same negative decisions repeatedly. Remember, the definition of insanity is doing the same thing over and over and expecting a different result. I don't believe this is actual insanity, but it can cause us to do the same thing over and over.

Let me give you a couple of personal examples. When I was about 10 years old, my mom took me to the state capitol in Topeka, KS. She wanted me to see the city from the dome of the Kansas State Capitol. That day it seemed that everyone wanted to do the same thing. So, we were maneuvering our way through a large crowd as we climbed the spiral stairway toward the top. I suddenly felt very closed-in and was having trouble breathing. Then I suffered a panic attack. From that day forward, I had difficulty being in crowds. Every time I was in a crowd, it triggered that tape, and I relived that event as if it were happening right then. But being in a crowd was not the only event that triggered a panic attack.

Thirteen years later in 1965, at the age of 23, I had my second panic attack, which was much more devastating to me. I was driving home from a sales meeting I'd attended in a town about 35 miles from where I lived. Suddenly, for no apparent reason, I began to feel very frightened. I began to sweat. I was breathing rapidly, and I began to shake all over. I honestly don't know how, but I finally made it home. For the next year, I was unable to leave my house unless someone was with me. It was humiliating, but the fear was just too great to overcome.

At the time, I was an insurance salesman. Obviously, I made a living getting out, meeting people, and making sales. Since I couldn't leave the house without feeling panicked, I did the next best thing. Being an independent agent, I set up an office in my house and ran my business from there. How did I make any sales you ask? Well, I did all my prospecting from home by telephone. I would then make the sale over the phone and get the client to come by my "home office" to fill out the paperwork. The upside of this was that I became a master at telephone prospecting and sales. I also honed my listening skills to where I could monitor the prospects moods and feelings by the tone of their voices.

Over time the humiliation and indignity of the situation began to weigh on me, and I felt that I had to fight back. One day I decided that I was going to go by myself to get a haircut. If what happened wasn't so serious it would have been hilarious. I'm almost ashamed to tell it. Anyway, I made it to the barbershop and nervously waited my turn.

Finally, I was in the chair and the barber was cutting my hair. He was about half finished when the panic attack hit me. I bolted from the chair, raced through the door, and went running down the street with the barber's apron still attached around my neck. It was flowing behind me like a cape. Fortunately, the barber caught up with me and retrieved his apron. Ultimately, I was able to return to the barbershop and get the rest of my haircut. It was one of the most embarrassing moments of my life.

Shortly after that humiliating experience, I finally couldn't take it anymore. I knew that I had to make a change in my life. I forced myself to push back the fear and get out of the house by myself. It was hard, but I just could not continue living with how I felt about myself.

It was in my early sessions with Coach that he gave me insights as to part of what was driving my panic attacks and how I'd chosen to fight them. He explained to me that survival is our strongest instinct. When we see or sense a perceived threat, we determine the level of the threat based on our level of security. If we feel very secure in our ability to handle the threat, we feel less fearful. When we feel insecure in our ability to handle it, our fear level rises.

In my case, he explained that in my youth my mother represented a major source of security. When she died, a lot of my sense of security was stripped away leaving me more susceptible to a high of level of fear. Since I'd never dealt with my feelings about her death, I'd never found a replacement for that part of my security.

Along with the insecurity resulting from my mother's death, I also possessed negative tapes that had a huge impact on my life. They resulted from rejection, especially rejection by women whom I cared for. Early in my relationship with Darlene, I found myself conflicted because I knew I loved her deeply but could not stop myself from worrying about her betraying me. She was a beautiful woman, and I couldn't believe that I deserved her.

One day, about a week after we met, I walked into the hotel where the Army was billeting students and instructors. I was heading for my room. As I turned the corner, I saw her standing in the hall talking with a fellow instructor, whom I didn't particularly like. That scene instantly triggered jealousy and anger. My mind immediately replayed old tapes complete with all the betrayal inflicted by other women in my life.

All the negative feelings and the fear I'd experienced came rushing back. Without bothering to check out the facts, I ran down the hallway and threw a punch towards the instructor's head. He ducked and my hand went through the sheetrock wall. After the facts were revealed, it became clear that the situation was not what it appeared. Darlene later told me that she realized then that she was going to need to spend a lot of time helping me learn to trust again.

Please don't misunderstand me. We record the happy positive events as well and relive those when they are triggered. For example, think for a moment about your wedding, your high school graduation, or any other significant event that you enjoyed. As soon as you picture it, you will start feeling the positive energy take hold. The memories of those events tend to enrich your life, making the journey seem worth the trouble. But what are triggers?

The most common triggers are connected to the five senses: sight, hearing, smell, taste and touch. For example, a song might remind you of someone you dated. Cologne or perfume might also remind you of a special person. Along with that memory comes an array of feelings that could be positive or negative. Seeing an old movie that reminds you of someone special is a powerful trigger because it transports you back to the memories of that special person for a longer time.

Darlene and I have several songs and a movie that are very special to us, and we love to watch and listen to those when we are going through negative times to help create positive energy flow. As I said before, the movie *"Honeysuckle Rose"* and the song *"On the Road Again,"* by Willie Nelson, are very special to us.

The movie and song are special for many reasons. Most importantly, the day we saw the movie was the first time we spent quality time together. Reliving that experience helps us to realize that we are committed to each other no matter what happens. In addition, the positive emotion of love generated by that event helps us make good decisions about our relationship.

I learned so many things from Coach over the years. But one of the most important things was that my decisions determine the direction of my life. Moreover, there are four things that determine how I make those decisions. Those four are:
1. How I feel about the situation.
2. The facts available to me.
3. The emotion to which those feelings are attached, positive or negative.
4. My past experiences in similar situations.

In each situation, it is critical to realize which emotion the feelings are attached to because that emotion, positive or negative, will determine the final decision. Therefore, it is necessary to learn to separate feelings from emotions. It takes awareness and practice.

For example, when I was a First Sergeant in the Army, I was assigned a new company commander. He was a young, newly promoted captain. One morning, when the company was assembled, he called one soldier out in front of the formation and rather strongly corrected him for a mistake he had made. I felt furious. All I wanted to do was dismiss the troops and drag him into his office and knock some sense into him. When we got back to the orderly room, I went into my office shut the door and tried to figure what I should do. I had to decide. Do I go in there and forcefully explain his mistake of reprimanding a soldier in public when it should have been done in private? Or do I cool down and let it pass? First, I knew that my feelings of absolute anger were coming from negative emotion, from fear. I feared the situation I might have to face if I acted; I feared that failing to act was shirking my duty as a First Sergeant. But most of all, I feared what could happen to my career because I was less than a year from retiring.

I thought hard about it. In conversations with other First Sergeants who'd faced the same situation, the majority had made the decision of confrontation. Some had problems afterwards; most did not. So, I decided to confront him with the intention of helping him to be a better leader. In other words, I was now operating out of the emotion of love rather than fear and I had control of my actions.

Nevertheless, this was the Army after all. So, this was not going to be a "honey you made a mistake," kind of discussion. There was always a risk confronting a commanding officer.

Here is what happened. I walked into his office and slammed the door, maybe a little too hard because his airborne plaque fell off the wall. But I had his attention. I walked up as close as I could to the front of his desk and leaned toward him.

"Sir," I said, "with all due respect, my job as your First Sergeant is twofold. First, it is to help you get promoted to Major. Second, it is to keep you from doing something stupid and being demoted to Lieutenant. What you did today correcting that soldier in front of his peers is high on the list of things not to do as a good leader. From this point on, we discuss the issues before a final decision is made. Is that clear, Sir?" He agreed.

We got along great after that. I don't know how much I influenced him as a leader, but I've been told that he ultimately retired as a Full Colonel.

So how does this apply to our everyday lives? Every day we are faced with many challenges that require making decisions. Some are more serious than others. But they are all important because they determine the direction of our lives and directly affect our emotional wellbeing.

I retired from the Army in January of 1989 and started my own company, providing training, consulting and coaching in the areas of relationship building, communication, sales, and leadership for multiple Fortune 500 companies. In addition, I became a professional speaker and joined the National Speakers Association (NSA). I was blessed to be able to achieve the Certified Speaking Professional (CSP) award. In the process, my new associations accelerated my learning. I had the opportunity to learn from the likes of Brian Tracy, Zig Ziglar (God bless him), and Og Mandino the author of *The Greatest Salesman in the World.*

After retiring, two major turning points in my life steered me on my beautiful journey to enlightenment.

Chapter 8

Core values determine what we consider to be right and wrong. When we make decisions contrary to those values, it affects us negatively. I'm convinced of this because I have experienced the transition from a life of fear, panic, and emotional turmoil to a life of joy, calm, and peace of mind. I did this by having learned how to make better decisions. I've learned why I make the decisions I make, which makes it possible for me to make more positive and effective decisions.

For example, have you ever seen something being done at work that was wrong? At that moment, you were faced with a very important decision. Do you report it, or do you look the other way and hope someone else will take care of it? If you decided to report the situation, you did it because your values and ethics played a strong role in making that decision. In addition, you probably realized that taking a stand in the past for what was right achieved mixed results, positive and negative.

If you looked the other way, most likely it was because you were afraid of the consequences of reporting it. Such consequences might include losing your job or being labeled a snitch. In my 22 years of coaching and training, I've seen many situations like this. Even in the executive suites, wrong decisions are made for the same reasons.

What I find even more disheartening is how this affects families. When one spouse does something that is counter to the overall good of the family, and the other spouse ignores the action, he/she is giving tacit approval. This could damage family trust.

Failing to be open and honest with your spouse and your children leads to bad behavior and distrust. What's worse, it often leads to the end of the marriage or relationship. I've seen this in my coaching with couples and individuals going through tough times. Fear impedes or stops the flow of honest communication. All too often, lack of honest communication leads to couples blaming each other for their problems, when they are both responsible for the breakdown.

Don't leave out the impact on the children. I have five children from two marriages. So, I have a little experience in that area. Believe me, I have made my share of mistakes. I do not claim to be an expert in raising children. God help parents who claim to be experts because the children will soon prove them wrong. But I do know that if you learn to manage your fear you will make much better decisions, which will encourage them to do the same.

This is not just for you, however. It is for your children as well, the future generations who will be tomorrow's world leaders. Think about it. It took you a lifetime to learn how to fear. Think of the countless decisions you have made based on fear and their outcomes. What if your children could learn at a young age that fear does not have to influence so many of their decisions. Wouldn't they be better off? After all, it is our responsibility as parents to teach and guide our children (no matter how old they are) and to show them the disciplines they need to live happier, more productive lives.

The point is that fear drives many parent/child relationships. Why? Here is an example. Many parents decide to provide a better life for their children than they had growing up. Both parents often work many hours with the intention of being the best providers they can be. But parents can go overboard in the process and lose sight of why they are raising children. Materialism can be addictive. They work so many hours to provide the material things that they believe their children need. Often, they don't see their children much during the week. Interestingly, a recent trend in our culture is for parents to encourage friendship over parenting to compensate for the lack of contact with their children. They become buddies. This can make it tougher for parents to dish out discipline when necessary, leading children to take advantage of their parents.

I believe that parents experience guilty feelings for not spending enough quality time with their children. Those feelings are attached to the emotion of fear. Therefore, often the decision to befriend their children is based on fear. As a result, children do not get the opportunity to learn discipline so critical to their growth and development. But don't think of discipline only as disciplinary action, such as a spanking. It can also mean being ready each day to get to the bus stop on time or turning in homework on time.

I know this from a bit of experience. There was a time in my training and coaching career that I had no work as an employee for about six months because I hadn't yet procured a contract necessary to work in my own business. I couldn't stay idle. So, I started substitute teaching. On my first day in the classroom, I was so appalled at the students' lack of self-discipline that I almost quit that day. But I hung in there. Maybe things would change, I thought.

By my third day, I changed the way I introduced myself to the class to try to inspire better general behavior. I introduced myself and then asked, "How many of you know what a First Sergeant is?" Believe it or not the majority did know! So, I asked them what a First Sergeant does, and they all said he is a real mean guy who does bad things to people. At that point, I gave them the same spiel that I gave every new troop that came into my company. I said, "I can be your best friend, or I can be your worst enemy, the decision is yours. Follow the rules and behave and we'll get along fine. Break the rules and you are going to have a problem. Is that clear?"

The change in their behavior amazed me after I laid out the rules. They appeared to appreciate discipline. They became curious about me and began asking questions. They would ask, "Why do we need to study this stuff? We'll never use it in real life." I heard that question enough to inspire me to formulate an exercise to help them understand why learning was important.

I broke them into small groups and gave them the assignment. For 15 minutes, they wrote down as many reasons as possible how using the material will help in some aspect of their lives after graduation. I was shocked at the response because nearly every group came up with at least one or two cases where they could use it.

Of course, there were times where I had to pull students aside and have heart to heart discussions about their behavior. Each time I did my best to determine why they misbehaved and tried to provide constructive suggestions to help them. Often, they thanked me for the discipline that I demanded of them. It's my opinion that most of our kids are acting out because they don't understand why they need to do certain things, and, most of all, because they are seeking discipline. I truly believe they are crying for help and guidance in a world that is offering them hundreds of conflicting messages.

I don't know how much overall value this was to the kids I had in class, but I know that two interesting things happened. First, kids started calling out to me and waving when they saw me on campus. Secondly, I began getting special requests which originated from students who'd asked that I substitute for their teachers.

As I have already said, our decisions determine the direction of our lives and emotions drive those decisions. So, to change or improve the direction our lives, we must learn how to handle our emotions, especially our fear. Coach spent a lot of time helping me to understand how to control my emotions. He helped me to understand that a lot of my feelings were generated by past events in my life. Consequently, if I could change how I perceived those events, or my connection to those events, it would change my feelings and lessen their impact on my current situation.

Coach taught me that since each event is recorded in pictures, complete with emotion and sound, it became real in the present even though it was in the past. He helped me to understand that the picture would never go away. It would always appear when triggered. However, it was possible to disconnect the emotion from the event so that, when the tape played, I would encounter the video of the event minus the feelings attached to it. There are various ways to accomplish this. The one he used most with me was writing a letter to the individual or to the event. I was so pleased with the results that I often ask my clients to do the same. Let me give you an example.

One day I walked into Coach's office for a session, and he hit me with a disturbing question, he said, "Nick, how do you feel about your mother?"

I was floored, as I hadn't consciously thought of her in years. I said, "I don't understand what you're asking because she passed away when I was 15 years old," I said.

Of course, when he asked the question, everything surrounding her death came rushing back in an instant as if I was there all over again. I remember the 3 a.m. call from the hospital saying she was near death. I remembered being the last one in her room holding her hand as she opened her eyes; she smiled at me and then passed. I remembered the funeral and all the people looking at us. I could smell the flowers. Then I was standing, looking down at her in the casket, seeing her for the last time. Then I collapsed, emotionally drained. Thankfully my uncle caught me, so I didn't fall. True to the male code, I didn't shed a tear in front of all those people. In fact, I never did shed a tear. Coach had patiently waited for me to process his question. Finally, I looked at him and said, "I really don't know how I feel after all these years."

He said, "Okay here is your assignment for our next session. I want you to sit down and write her a letter telling her how you feel about her. Don't do this on your computer. Do it with a pencil and paper. Don't hold back your feelings. Be honest about how you feel."

Boy, what an assignment. I let it set for a couple of days and then started writing. I was amazed at the things coming out of my mind and mouth. I was using words like, "I'm so totally angry with you for leaving me," and that is the mildest of it. Yes, there were some curse words in there also. The venom coming out in my feelings was almost scaring me. I finished with three full pages.

The next week I walked into our session with my letter and gave it to Coach. He handed it back to me and said, "I don't want it. I want you to read it aloud to me."

I started reading and immediately started to break down. Tears flowed uncontrollably down my face. It took me nearly forty minutes to finish the three pages. When I was done, Coach simply looked at me and said, "How did you sign it?"

I looked at him and said, "I didn't sign it." He looked at me and asked why. I didn't have an answer.

He told me there could be several reasons, one of which was I had more to say. But he explained that it was important for me to sign it because a signature signified closure to the letter. "Take it home," he said. "Finish it and then sign it for next week." I waited until the night before my meeting with him before I added a couple of lines and signed it.

The next morning, I walked into his office, and he told me to read the letter again. I did and it only took a couple of minutes. He sat silent for a few minutes waiting for me to do something. Finally, "Aren't you going to read your signature?" he asked. I looked down at my signature and as I started to read it, I completely lost it. Honestly, it took me the rest of the session to get the words completely out.

The feeling that rushed over me was like nothing I'd ever experienced in my life. The only way I can explain it is that my whole life had changed in an instant and would never be the same. Picture an inbox on your desk filled with organized work. Suddenly someone put their hands under the pile and threw it up in the air. Paper was flying everywhere. The papers were the details of my life completely out of order never to return to the same order. As I calmed down Coach sent me home for the rest of the day.

At the time Darlene was working. So, the house was quiet and still. I walked into the living room, turned on the TV, sat on the floor and leaned back against the sofa holding the letter, staring into space sobbing. Later that afternoon I became aware of Darlene asking me if I was okay. I was oblivious to the fact that she had returned from work. She came and sat on the sofa rubbing my shoulders. She asked about the meeting with Coach, and I told her what happened, adding that he had asked me to read the letter to my mother over her grave the next time we went back to my hometown.

But my wonderful, brilliant wife had an idea. She told me to stand up, bring my letter, and follow her. We got in the car, and she drove to a nearby cemetery. She stopped in front of a headstone saying "Mother" and told me to go sit beside it and read the letter. I did. It was much easier this time and only took a few minutes. When we got home, I immediately went to bed and fell into a deep sleep.

This exercise worked for me. The next morning, I slowly opened my eyes and saw the sunlight shining through the blinds and across my bed. The smell of the fresh spring air flowing through the open window was sweet and refreshing. As I awoke, I felt refreshed and had a deep sense that something was significantly different. I'd never ever felt this way before. My body felt light as a feather, and I was tingling with an excitement that bordered on euphoria. As I sat up, I shouted, "Oh my God, this is a feeling that no one will ever be able to take away from me. This truly is the first day of the rest of my life."

What was this feeling I was experiencing? Then gently it settled into my conscious mind. This feeling is peace, deep lasting peace, the kind of peace that makes life like heaven on earth. It's the peace that finally, in my troubled life, gave understanding to the words Jesus said to his disciples, *"Peace I leave with you; my peace I give you."*

I realize that not everyone is going to experience what I experienced writing that letter to my mother for a variety of different reasons. In my case, this event had happened nearly forty years earlier and was deeply buried in my subconscious mind. It had been a determining factor in my view on life and I never realized it. Unfortunately, most of my decisions in one way or another were deeply influenced by that event.

Results of writing letters may vary depending on how deep the issue is and the level of emotion attached to it. It may take more than one letter to the same person to disconnect the emotion from the event. If you remember earlier in my story, I told how the bully in high school nearly suffocated me. The emotion from that event was so deep seeded that it took three different letters to the bully before I could disconnect the emotion from that event. It is important to know that you don't need to send the letter to the other person. Writing and reading a letter will do the trick. Sending the letter might do more harm than good, especially if the other party doesn't even remember the event or events that caused the trauma.

As our sessions continued, Coach explained that at birth our spirit shines brightly. It is innocent and fresh. But life's constant challenges cast shadows over the brightness of our spirit. Over the years, the shadows build and build and weigh us down. To reclaim the brightness of our spirit, we must peel those negative shadows back one at a time until our spirit is bright and shining again. He explained that my mother's untimely, unexpected death was the first major challenge to hit my young life.

Unfortunately, her death became a mostly negative guiding factor in my life even though I was totally unaware of it. I didn't realize it at the time, but it was the first time I questioned God's love and distrusted him because he allowed my mother to die.

Hindsight, of course, is 20/20. Now, as I look back on it, I see His wisdom and how He guided me toward my mission. I would not be doing what I'm doing today if I hadn't experienced the challenges in my life and His guidance in handling them. To me, that is what is meant when we say by God's Grace. It took me many years to learn that. But it was a lesson well learned. Now I must share what I know with others. That is my mission. I share this information in coaching sessions with my clients, in conversations with my friends and family and through this book.

Chapter 9

I've learned from experience that writing letters can be very useful for so many issues. But I also learned that there are other tools for removing the power that the past has over us and the role it plays in keeping our fears alive and well.

Before I go into those, however, I want to share with you one piece of wisdom that Coach gave me. To this day it has helped me immensely. At one point, I was experiencing a lot of fear and struggling with my reaction to it both physically and emotionally.

One morning, he asked me if I'd ever ridden a roller coaster. I chuckled and said, "Hasn't everybody?" He asked me to tell him how it made me feel. "That's simple," I said. "It was very exciting. In fact, the first time I rode one was at an amusement park in Chicago in 1982. I was scared to death during the long wait to get on the ride." I told Coach that once the ride was over, I was so excited that I got back in line to ride it again.

Coach then explained my rationale for wanting to ride the roller coaster again even though at first, I was afraid to ride it. *He said that the physical response I felt before (fear) and afterwards (excitement) were the same.* In both cases, I would experience an increased heart rate, elevated blood pressure and possible increased perspiration and breathing. Then he shocked me. He said the difference in the two situations was the way you labeled the feelings you were experiencing. When I labeled it fear, questioning whether I was going to survive the ride, it was a negative energy, which produced negative stress. However, when I labeled it excitement, I generated positive energy that resulted in positive stress and a positive experience.

Furthermore, he said that less than ten percent of what we fear ever comes to pass. But worrying about it doesn't help. In fact, worry and doubt can cause it to happen because our negative energy increases the chances of facing exactly what we feared the most. In other words, we draw negative energy to us. It's called the self-fulfilling prophecy.

I finally realized that I am truly the captain of my ship, the master of my life. I control the direction of my life, regardless of what is going on around me, unless I give that control over to something or someone else. I learned that my perceptions are my reality, and I label those realities as good, bad or what I expected. Coach explained that we all have expectations of what our lives should and should not be. If our lives are going along as expected, we're okay and we label them that way. If we are doing better than we expected, we feel ecstatic and label ourselves as terrific. Our self-confidence and emotional wellbeing soar off the chart. Positive energy abounds. However, if we are not where we expected to be, we tend to label ourselves as failures. Our self-confidence drops and negative energy floods us.

Unfortunately, often we set our expectations higher than the knowledge, skill, and ability we possess at that point in our lives. Let me give you an example of what I experienced myself.

When I was a freshman in college, I was enrolled in a world history class. I considered myself a pretty good student of history and my expectation was to be number one in that course. Unfortunately, there was another student in the class who was a retired navy chief who had traveled the world for twenty years. I guess I don't need to tell you who came in first in the class, do I? It sure wasn't me. I immediately labeled myself a failure. The fact is that I was not a failure. I had simply set my expectations beyond my experience and knowledge at the time. What I've learned to understand is that being surpassed in this situation didn't in any way make me a failure. My competitive nature made me a better student and I'm sure I got a better grade than I would have if it hadn't been striving so hard to be number one.

One day Coach asked me if I was getting a better understanding of how all those negative events from my past were having a negative impact on my present. I told him that I did and that it was helping me a lot to have that understanding. He then shared with me that the more negative events I held on to, the more they dragged me down and damaged my ability to take advantage of the many opportunities that came my way.

He told me that one of the keys to achieving my goals and living a much happier life was to remove those little balls of crap from my mind and lighten my load. He said that in addition to writing the letters, I needed to stop living in the past or the future and start living in the present. I wasn't sure what he meant. He explained that when we look to the past for guidance we are living in the past. When we look to the future for guidance we are living the future. Unfortunately, the past can't be changed. It's over and the future isn't here yet. So, you are living your life in a "shoulda," "woulda," "coulda" world.

I challenged him. "How can that be? If I forget the past, I'll just make the same mistakes again and again. I've got to hang on to it and study it deeply, so I don't make the same mistakes."

He smiled with a gentle caring look as he always had. "Nick", he said, "Let me explain something to you about the role our past plays in our lives. Each minute of our lives is like a snowflake; it is different than any other minute in our life. As that minute passes, it becomes part of our past and cannot be changed, altered or done over. Therefore, it is important that you realize that the past is past. You no longer have control over it. But here is the key you need to understand and why it's okay to let go of the past.

"You learn from the events you experience, and you carry that knowledge with you, and expand on it as you continue in life. Don't worry about what you didn't learn because it will come around again and again, disguised differently, of course, until you learn what you needed to know. You must realize that every day we learn more and understand more. Understand that the reason you didn't learn everything you needed is because you weren't ready to learn it yet. Think about it. Haven't you ever had a moment when you suddenly said, 'oh, now I get it, why didn't I see it before?' I'm sure you have had those. We all do. That is the point that you had learned enough and gained enough experience to recognize what you needed to know.

"Here is what I want you to do that will help you to move from the past into the present. First," he said, "I'm going to teach a relaxation exercise and then I'm going to give you a suggestion while you're in a relaxed state."

Here is the relaxation exercise he gave me. I sit in a comfortable chair, a recliner if possible. Otherwise, I sit in a chair with my feet on the floor. I close my eyes and take two or three deep breaths. As I take slow deep breaths, I start saying to myself, "I'm feeling more and more relaxed, stress is leaving me and I'm going deeper into relaxation. I feel the stress leaving my body and I'm feeling a deep sense of peace and calm."

Then I tell myself the following: "The past is past, and it can't be changed or altered. Let go of the past. Anything that I didn't learn will come around again and give me the opportunity to learn what I need to know. Remember, the past is past. Look forward to the future. It is beautiful and full of promise. But it is still in the future; therefore, I live in the present, the here and now. There are many wonderful opportunities available for me to consider and I make my decisions based on what I know at this time. If they take me where I want to go, I'm very happy. If they don't, I will make a new decision based on new information.

"On the count of five I'll be wide awake feeling refreshed and feeling a deep sense of peace and calm. One; Two; Three, I feel myself awakening; Four, I'm moving my feet, arms, and legs; Five, I'm wide-awake feeling calm, peaceful, and rested."

I also repeated this suggestion to myself three times a day and I began to realize that things were changing. Here is an example. I know you will think it is silly, but it had a big impact on me. After about three weeks of this relaxation exercise, repeating the suggestion several times a day, I was driving to a seminar that I was to conduct. As I drove along the interstate on a fall day, I suddenly realized that I was looking at the trees and bushes along the highway and admiring their beauty. Then I noticed the little things my wife did for me. I noticed that her mannerisms and actions were not only endearing to me but helped me relieve stress. In essence, I was feeling less stress, and I was enjoying my life more than ever before.

I must share with you that in the early stages of my journey back to God, my military counselor recommended a book for me to read that was a great help to me. The book is entitled, *"Why am I afraid to tell you who I am?"* The author is John Powell, Jesuit Priest and PhD. Powell explains why we are afraid to open up and make ourselves vulnerable to others. He also shares the importance of reporting our emotions to others as soon as it is appropriate. I don't know how many times I read that book, but I wore it out and had to get a new copy. It was my constant companion. At Fort Devens there was a beautiful, peaceful lake surrounded by woods. I would sit on the shore and read that book. The more I read the more I relaxed. I now realize that the reason it is so important to express our emotions is because they are what drive our decisions and our lives.

Now I share that book with my clients, and I explain its importance.

Let me share with you how I perceive the importance of opening ourselves up and being vulnerable. We all have things that we do not want anyone to know about us for a variety of reasons. Maybe we are ashamed of something we've done or maybe we're afraid of what people will think of us or what might happen to us if the secret ever got out. I see it as having this "secrets vault" inside our mind where we store all our private secrets and feelings that are never to be divulged.

We keep them so locked up that we expend a lot of energy to protect them. Therefore, we are rewarded with a lot of negative stress for our efforts. As a result, when we are with others, even our friends and spouses, we never let our guard down. As a result, there is always a wall between our loved ones and us. Unfortunately, this wall prevents us from having honest and open relationships. The truth, however, is that at some point something will slip, and the secret comes out causing problems in the relationship. Often these are issues of trust. Here is another way that lack of transparency damages relationships and our own peace of mind. When our secret is threatened, we tell a lie to protect it. Later it's threatened again, and we tell a lie to cover the original lie and ultimately, we can't remember what we told to whom and the stress ratchets up. I know because I have lived it. Earlier I told you the story of my panic attack in flight school and how couldn't fly after that. Well, that was not the original story that I told others for years. Here was the story I told to protect the secret I had locked in my secrets vault. When asked why I didn't finish flight school, I had two stories that I used to hide my feelings of failure, shame, and weakness for having panic attacks.

The first version was that I had a bad landing one day and messed up one of Uncle Sam's helicopters. So, the army decided to ground me. In this version, I was putting the blame on someone else. The second version was that President Nixon was scaling down the number of American pilots in favor of South Vietnamese pilots and they didn't need me to fly. Shortly after that came an actual reduction of pilots, which gave an element of truth to my story. It wasn't totally true, but not totally false either, a gray area.

It was a great lie I used to prevent my fear of truth from coming out. Anyway, one day Darlene accompanied me on my visit with Coach. I don't remember the conversation, but without thinking I blurted out the truth of the situation and Darlene's mouth dropped open. She'd never heard the truth. I simply dropped my head in shame, partly for why I hadn't finished flight school, but more so because I'd lied to those whom I should have trusted the most.

Yes, folks I told you in the Forword that I was going to be as transparent as possible. I'm human and some secrets may remain unconsciously hidden in my secrets vault. In fact, I know that's true because occasionally, I'll remember something that I've never told Darlene. I immediately share it with her even though sometimes it is very difficult and painful. Honesty is always in style but it's not always easy. We both believe that for our relationship to remain strong we must not intentionally withhold any secrets.

So, is being vulnerable worth the emotional pain that might come with it? Well, that is certainly a decision you will need to make for yourself. From my point of view and experience, you'll never reach the level of personal peace you desire until you handle those secrets. There is a great country song that says, *"What she doesn't know won't hurt her but it's destroying me."* That's the way it is for all of us who believe that myth because we struggle with the guilt and the stress of keeping secrets, which separates us from our relationships.

As Coach shared this information about secrets and being open and honest, it made a lot of sense to me. So, I asked him how to open up and become more vulnerable. I should have known the answer, but he just gave me that little quirky smile and let me have it.

He started with a question. "Why do you hide your secrets and resist being vulnerable?" My obvious answer was that I was afraid of what would happen if the secret got out or if I allowed myself to be vulnerable. People would take advantage of me, and I'd get hurt.

He told me that fear is why we resist vulnerability. Therefore, the only way to be able to be totally open and honest is to learn to master fear and not let it control our lives. At that point he took me right back to the definition of fear; fear is a question. That question is, *"Am I going to be okay?"* The answer is always *'yes'* because God gave me the skill, knowledge, and ability to handle whatever happens.

However, he told me that I couldn't fully control the fear in my life until I could truly believe that statement in my heart. It's easy to believe it intellectually, but when the crap hits the fan, you forget it. It only stays with you when you truly believe it. So how do you move your belief from your head to your heart? The answer is one word: Faith. I believe we all have faith in something. Unfortunately, we often put our faith in things and people that let us down.

In my opinion, there are three things in which we can put our faith. First, we have faith in ourselves. Again unfortunately, we often find it

116

hard to have complete faith in ourselves because we often question and second-guess ourselves.

Second, we have faith in our fellow man. I believe that most of us would agree that putting faith in people doesn't always work out the way we plan. In my opinion, we put more faith in people than in God or ourselves. I suppose that is because we believe we can trust them and that we can have some control over them. We know that we have no control over God.

Third, we have faith in God. Over my years of coaching, most people have told me that they find it hard to seriously have deep faith in God. When I ask them why, they give me one of two reasons. First, they don't see His actions on their behalf. Secondly, when they pray, their prayers sometimes go unanswered. Some of you may feel the same way. I know I did after all the enormous challenges I have faced. Thankfully, I've now come to realize that God answers every prayer. Before you dismiss that comment, let me explain what Coach helped me to understand. Our prayers are often a request for help in some situation we are experiencing. They spell out what we want and therein is the breakdown.

Coach helped me to understand that God answers every prayer, but he always gives what we need, not necessarily what we want. Since we don't like the answer, we blame Him for not answering our prayer. What Coach helped me to do was to watch what happened after I offered up my prayer to see if the situation had changed. If nothing happened, he told me that I needed to continue doing what I was doing while looking for ways to improve the situation. If something changes, I should examine it and decide how to integrate it into my life.

He also pointed out that many of our prayers are answered in how we perceive our situation. I have experienced these many times over the years. I have found it amazing that when my perception about a challenge changed, I went from being a victim to a victor. Yes, it can be difficult to go from victim to victor because that is often outside of our comfort zone. We all need help in this area. We often can't do it alone. My wife and I have helped each other through many such experiences. One that comes to mind happened in the fall of 1998.

Our speaking and training business was doing very well. In fact, I had all of 1999 booked and was looking at a solid six figure income that year. We had an opportunity to sell our house in Powder Springs, GA, just west of Atlanta. Darlene and I had been thinking about relocating to Florida. She wanted to move back to Florida where she had lived before enlisting in the army, and I liked the idea of being close to the ocean.

We found a beautiful house in the little town of Oviedo, FL, which is just outside of Orlando.

In fact, we thought it might end up being our retirement home. We moved into our new house two days before Thanksgiving 1998. We'd spent quite a bit of money making the move but weren't worried because we had a great year booked for 1999.

Once again, however, life got in the way, one more challenge to face and learn from. Two weeks before Christmas, I got a call from the company that I was scheduled to train for the next year with less than good news. It seems that the company was experiencing some financial difficulties, and they had canceled all outside training until further notice. Wow! That was a real punch in the financial gut. I was very upset and worried about our finances. Yes, I knew that fear was a question, and I knew that we'd be okay. Like any traumatic event in our lives, this one staggered me, and I allowed fear to gain the upper hand.

One evening Darlene and I were sitting in the living room lost in our own thoughts and looking at the beautiful Christmas tree, which was devoid of presents. To say the least, I was depressed and struggling with what I considered my inability to provide for my family.

Suddenly Darlene got to her feet and said she'd be right back. I wasn't sure what she was doing, but I continued in my funk knowing that this was going to defiantly be a "hard candy"

Christmas. After a short time, she returned to the room carrying three beautifully wrapped boxes. "What are those?" I asked, knowing that we hadn't bought any gifts. With a big smile on her face, she explained the gifts one by one as she placed them under the tree.

The first box she explained is FAITH. She said that no matter how bad things got we must hold on to our faith. We need our faith in God and in ourselves to persevere in hard times. She said that faith was so critical because without it there is no hope. She then pointed out that without God and our faith in Him we would not have the second gift.

The second box was labeled LOVE. Love she said is so important because love comes directly from God because God is love. We must love God with all our heart and soul because it is from Him that we receive our strength. We must love each other and not allow negative circumstances to ever come between us and cause us to ever doubt or question our total dedication, devotion, and love for each other.

The third box said HOPE. Because of the faith and love we have for Him, and for each other, we are given the third gift, the gift of hope. Without faith and love, there would be no hope. Without hope there can be no tomorrow.

With that she came and held me and said, "This is going to be a great Christmas sweetheart because we have God, we have each other, and we have hope." As I stood there with tears streaming down my face, I felt like a King. There was nothing on earth more important to me at that moment than this beautiful woman and the wonderful life that we shared.

It is now twenty years later and every Christmas those three wonderful gifts are the first to be placed under our Christmas tree. Yes, there are other gifts, which are very nice and appreciated, but none are as important to us as "The Three Boxes."

Chapter 10

So, in January of 1999, I struck out in search of some sort of employment that would sustain us while I looked for new contracts. Fortunately, I was able to get a part time job selling major appliances for a major retailer. It was a start but not enough to keep us going. I continued to look for additional opportunities and was able to find a position as a substitute teacher. Between the two, we were able to meet most of our basic expenses but fell behind on several of our obligations.

Later in the year we received a package in the mail from NSA (National Speaking Association) friends. We opened it and found a small book, *"The Prayer of Jabez,"* with a note. It told us to read the book and say the prayer at least once a day for thirty days. In addition, the note instructed us not to contact them until the end of the thirty days. We were instructed to wait and see what happened in our lives during that time.

We did what our friends requested. I was amazed when two weeks later I received a call from a colleague telling me that he had set up an interview for me the following Friday in Tampa. I met with representatives of a major Fortune 50 company looking to secure a trainer for a long-term contract, which paid extremely well.

I got the contract, and it lasted until the end of 2010. What a blessing it turned out to be! It enabled us to get our finances back on track and to take care of my aging father both financially and medically until he passed away in late August of 2010.

I recommend this book to my clients, and I encourage you to read it as well. Those who have accepted my recommendation to pray the prayer daily have had something good happen in their lives. To this day we pray that prayer every morning and every evening.

In fact, here is the prayer I say every night before I go to sleep: The first four lines of this prayer are the prayer of Jabez. The rest is my personal prayer.

Oh, Lord that you would bless me indeed
And enlarge my territory.
Oh, that your hand would be with me and
Keep me from evil that it not
Cause me pain.
Jesus, I love you very much and put everything into your hands.
Thank you for giving me strength, knowledge, and wisdom
To make it through each day and protect me through these
Very difficult, challenging, and dangerous times.
Jesus, I believe that through you I will always have divine guidance

That I will always take the right turn in the road.
I believe that God will always find a way where
there is no way, and
If God is for us who can be against us?
I believe I can do all things through Christ which
strengthens me and I
Believe that if I have faith nothing is impossible
to me.
Amen

In November of 2010 it was time to renew my long-term contract. Unfortunately, the company was going to require me to continue working in a location away from home for extended periods of time. This caused me major concern because over the years I'd spent an inordinate amount of time traveling to ensure a steady and sufficient income to cover our needs. Frankly both of us had reached the point that it was a sacrifice that neither of us was willing to continue making. The decision we faced was simple; renew the contract and live separately for a year or decline it and take a chance of finding something closer to home. You need to understand that our love for each other, and being together is extremely important to us, more so than money.

Since my father had passed away our expenses had declined significantly. We decided to decline the contract and look for something without the travel. It appeared to be the best decision based on our circumstances and the information we had at the time.

Our plan was to take a small second mortgage on the house to tide us over until I had a new local contract. By our calculations, we had over $200,000 equity in the property. However, we discovered that because of the recession, we did not have the equity we thought we had. In fact, we were upside down by about $48,000. There is an adage with regard to making plans, "Man plans, and God laughs."

So here we were again, no work and very little money. Wow we've been here before. Yes, I know many of you are saying that we made a really bad decision by not renewing the contract. Many years ago, I'd have agreed with you and beat myself up furiously for being so stupid. But I'd learned that we make neither good nor bad decisions. We only make decisions and then label them good or bad based on their outcomes. This one just did not get us what we wanted. Instead of beating ourselves up and becoming additional victims of the great recession, we chose to make a new decision based on new information. It was faith, love, and hope that gave us the strength to accomplish this. But by now we understood that every challenge we faced provided us with the opportunity to learn another life lesson and strengthen our relationship with God. We also knew that we could handle it, and we would be okay. Even armed with this knowledge, it's still a challenge and it's still a struggle to work your way through it.

We prayed for help in determining how we were going to handle our current dilemma while we continued to work on a solution. Of course, when you are trying to work through a major challenge, if anything can go wrong it will. As it turned out, we lost it all, car, home, everything and our credit scores dropped like a rock. I could be mad at God for not giving us what we prayed for. Instead, it was time to figure out what He gave us that we needed.

A big door had slammed in our faces. I know you've all heard it said that when one door closes another one opens. Well, that's true, but the new door doesn't always swing open wide. It opens just a crack so that we need to look for it. To be able to see it, however, we can't be clouded by fear, anger, and worry. Remember we're going to be okay. We're going to find a way to handle the situation because we've got the skill, knowledge, and ability to do so. Remember, God will never give us a heaver load to carry than He gives us the strength to carry it.

There is a caveat to that; however, He gives the strength to carry the load for this day's challenges not for all the crap we insist on dragging with us for years. This is another reason to live in the present and let go of the past. There is no need to carry around the past because it is a burden that weighs you down on the journey of life.

The point of this story is that God answered our prayer by giving us what we needed not what we wanted. The gift He gave us was the small crack in the open door. As we evaluated our situation, we began to see it from a new perspective and made the decision to make what we refer to as our *"Beverly Hillbillies"* move to Arizona in January 2011.

It was an emotional task as we went through all our possessions and divided them into three piles, Goodwill, Arizona and trash. The Arizona pile we packed into a 26-foot U-Haul truck and headed west with our belongings and our kittens. Why did we choose to do that? First, Darlene's parents lived there and were getting older and we wanted to help them, if we could. Second, it is less expensive to live in Arizona than in Florida.

Our lifestyle had changed. But after much reflection, I began to realize that God was trying to tell me something and I hadn't yet figured out what it was. I also realized that even though we possessed very little materially, we did have the most important things in life and that they were not material possessions. They were faith, hope, and love. Embracing them, we began to more fully appreciate what we had. There is an old saying that goes like this, "I felt sorry for myself because I had no shoes until I saw a man who had no feet."

So now we are settled in Arizona living on my Army Retirement and Social Security, which was less than 50,000 dollars a year and certainly a far cry from our previous six-figure income. Now what? To be honest, because of all the years of being on the road and the schedule I'd kept, I was physically exhausted. Both Darlene and I had been worn out by the stress of the past months since my father's death. So, we decided to take time to unwind, relax, and enjoy just being together without the need to have an everyday schedule. We spent the entire year of 2011 recovering physically, mentally, and spiritually.

You may be wondering about the bills that we had before we moved to Arizona. That is a great question. Certainly, there was no way we could make the payments. Most of the debt was unsecured in the form of credit cards. Here is what we did. We own a service called LegalShield, which for less than 40 dollars a month, provides us with access to the best law firms in the country. We contacted our local law firm. With guidance from our attorneys, we were able to keep the harassing phone calls and letters to a minimum. We were extremely relieved when we learned what our rights were when it came to the issue of debt.

It was during that year that a small door opened causing us to look at our situation from a different perspective. Meanwhile, the crack began to open wider. Deep down I kept having this nagging feeling that there was something I was missing and that I needed to know. As the days and months passed, I realized that there was something I was trying to remember. Then one morning when I awoke it was right there. It was an event that happened many years before.

The event occurred in November of 1992 when I had the opportunity to work with a colleague of Zig Ziegler's in Shephard, TX. During my speaking career, Zig had mentored me on several occasions. His colleague, Jaunell Teague, had a program for helping professional speakers drill down and find their unique talent so they could mold it into their messages. It was a grueling three-day course. The days were long and there was homework in the evening. Late in the afternoon of the third day, she asked me why I interacted with people the way I do. Without thinking I gave her a response that lasted for several minutes.

When I finished, both her and Darlene – who had sat in on the training with me – were sitting there with their mouths open. She asked me where I had learned that, and I said I had no idea. She simply blurted out, "Your talent is your ability to read *'human energy'*."

At that time, I had no understanding of what *'human energy'* was. I've since come to realize that we all have some level of understanding regarding the feelings of others. In my case, I had an extremely high sensitivity to what others were feeling. I can pass someone in a shopping mall or on the street and sense how they feel. Honestly, this is both a blessing and a curse. Now don't misunderstand me. This is not something that makes me better than anyone else. It is the unique talent that God gave to me. We all have special God-given talents and it's a matter of whether we use them or not. In my opinion, they are God's gifts to us. When we use them, it is our gift back to God.

Let me give you an example. A few years ago, I was in the hospital for several days. On the second or third day a doctor came to see me. As she was examining me, I got a strong feeling that something was wrong even though she was smiling and upbeat. Without thinking, I said to her, "I sense that you are struggling with something, and I want you to know that no matter what happens, you will be able to handle it because you have the skill and knowledge to do so. Remember, you are a very special and unique person. You deserve the best life has to offer and God will hold you and help you with every struggle in your life."

She stopped the exam, looked me in the eye, and quietly said, "Thank you so much. I really needed that today." She turned and quickly left the room as a tear began to roll down her cheek.

I lay there for a few minutes realizing what I'd just done. It was something that I never even thought of or planned, I just did it. My roommate looked at me and said, "Wow I've never heard that before. Does it apply to me as well?" I looked back at him and assured him that it did.

On the last day of training, Jaunell gave me a book that I still read and that I recommend to my clients as well. The book is *"God Calling,"* edited by A.J. Russell. Russell explains that it was written by two poor and courageous women who were fighting against sickness and poverty, facing a hopeless future. One of them even longed to be gone from this world. He (the living Christ) spoke with them every day. They then anonymously shared these conversations with Russell who published them in his book. I personally found this book valuable in helping me work through challenges.

Many times, I have awakened in the middle of the night worrying about one thing or another and found it impossible to go back to sleep. I came to a point where every time that happened, I would pick up the book and I would find myself relaxing and falling back to sleep. The story gave me hope and eased my worried mind.

As I remembered this event from 1992, I kept wondering what it was that was so important that it came back to me so vividly? I'd never really understood what it meant when Jaunell said, "I read human energy." What was that? The more I thought about it the more intrigued I became.

Over the next few years, the whole concept of human energy started to become clearer. My son Chris is a nuclear engineer. Over the years, he has taught me about energy. But I had never considered it in the context of the human condition. However, I was familiar with the importance of balancing body, mind, and spirit. So, I began there. What if we looked at the body, mind, and spirit as different forms of energy: physical energy, intelligent energy, and spiritual energy? We know from physics that energy can neither be created nor destroyed; it can only change form. The more I thought about it the clearer it became.

We each have a certain amount of energy that powers our body, mind, and spirit. Also, it shifts form from one area to another when needed. For example, remember the last time you were sick with a bad cold. You probably found that your mind didn't seem to function as well, and you were probably down in the dumps. It is my opinion that was because a large portion of your energy shifted to help fight the attack on the body thus affecting your thinking and your spirit.

132

The thing I couldn't yet understand was how this applied to the spirit. I knew that we have emotional energy, but I couldn't yet connect that to spiritual energy. The more I thought about it the more I became convinced that human energy is a unique integration of intelligent energy, physical energy, and emotional energy. I was still struggling to make the connection between emotional energy and spiritual energy. That was to come in the form of a life-altering event.

On Saturday morning December 12, 2015, I left home for an all-day business training. The meeting was great, and I arrived home happy and excited. That evening, I went into my home office and began to catch up on some computer work. Suddenly, I began to feel as though I was going to pass out. Everything in my field of vision began to dim except for a bright light directly in front of me. I felt it was drawing me into it, and it made me feel so good and relaxed that I wanted to walk into it. I'd never felt so calm and peaceful. Suddenly it was gone. Everything around me was back to normal and I felt a little disappointed. I felt fine so I kept working on my project for a while longer. Later I went into our enclosed patio where Darlene was and asked her what was for dinner. Then I told her what had happened. Obviously, she didn't take it quite the same way I did and insisted on rushing me to the hospital. I didn't think it was necessary. I was feeling fine, but she insisted on going.

When we got to the emergency room, doctors gave me a thorough exam and said they couldn't find anything that could have caused the issue. But they decided to keep me overnight for observation. I was against it, but I was overruled. The next morning was Sunday. So, I didn't expect much to happen because I was feeling well, and all my vitals were normal. I was wrong. Before 7 a.m., I got a visit from a representative of the company that manufactured the pacemaker I'd had for over seven years.

She hurried into my room and interrogated my pacemaker. I asked her how it looked, and she just smiled and left the room. In less than ten minutes the nurse came rushing in with a bag of something she was hooking up to my intravenous. She laid several sheets of paper on the bed and asked me to look at them before she turned on the medication. One look at the sheets got my attention. It was a list of all the ways the medication could kill me. I looked at her like she was crazy and said, "I'm not letting you turn that on. I feel fine."

She didn't say a word, turned, and left the room. Moments later the phone beside my bed rang. It was my doctor. He got right to the point; he asked me if I had any idea what had happened to me the night before. I told him no. He told me that I'd had a lethal ventricular tachycardia or v-tach. I asked what that was. He explained how the lower heart goes out of rhythm and clenches up. "What you need to know," he said, "is that last night you were only seconds away from death."

At that moment the one thing that I remembered was the very bright light I saw and how badly I wanted to go into it but was stopped. I wasn't afraid of dying, but I realized it must not be my time. I looked at the nurse, who had returned, and said, "Turn that thing on." The doctor told me he'd see me later in the day and he hung up.

I lay there thinking about what had happened in the last few hours and realized; I hadn't really been aware of how much my view on life had changed in the previous years. Only a few years earlier, I'd have freaked out if a doctor had told me that I was only seconds away from death. Even though I felt that I had a pretty good handle on how to control my fear, I now realized that I felt no fear from this traumatic incident.

Over the next several days, they ran every test there was on my heart and cardiovascular system. One morning, the doctor came to see me and told me that physically my heart was sound and that it was much like that of a 35-year-old athlete. Thank God for all those years of running. However, he pointed out that I had some electrical issues that needed to be addressed. Since my old pacemaker was over seven years old, he wanted to replace it with a defibrillator/pacemaker. Unfortunately, there was some difficulty with the insurance because of my age and not doing anything to prolong life. It was something about the new health care rules, I guess. The good news is that he found a way to get it approved and I'm now the proud owner of a new defibrillator/pacemaker.

After the surgery I went home. But I soon realized that I didn't have the stamina I'd previously had. It was then that I discovered that it would probably take some time for me to get all my stamina and strength back and that there was a psychological issue as well. In fact, I experienced some depression for a short time. It appears that when you are that close to death you subconsciously come face to face with your own mortality. It can be a shock to your body. I began to realize I was not ten feet tall and bullet proof.

As time went on, I began to realize that regardless of the situation, the core answer to the issues we face was always the same. The answer to the problem is to identify the fear and take control of it so that we can properly evaluate the situation. This stabilizes our instinctive fight or flight response and enables us to evaluate the situation and make the best decision we can with the information available to us. We must always remember that decisions made from fear often tend to give us unwanted results.

Several weeks after my brush with death, I began to fully realize that through the entire episode I never once experienced fear. I felt nothing but peace and calm. I also realized that all the things I'd learned over the preceding years were now very clear. I not only understood them better, but now I understood why they were so important for me to know. I realized that it was my mission in life to help those who were willing to share their feelings with me. It was clear that I had an ability to see their situations clearly and help them find solutions.

For example, one day over coffee, a couple shared with me some difficulties they were having in their relationship. Initially, the couple did not understand that their individual fears were the core of the problem. As Coach had shared with me many times, people don't connect their feelings with their emotions. In this case, the couple was making decisions based on their feelings without realizing that their individual fears had generated those feelings.

We talked for a short while and we were able to identify which fears had generated their feelings. Once that was done, we talked about the definition of fear and how through their faith they would be able to handle it because through their faith they would master their fear. Obviously, I can't reveal what they went through or the outcome because of confidentiality. But I can tell you that today I am very happy and proud of where they are in their lives.

As I progressed in my coaching, I started getting feedback from those that I'd spoken with thanking me for the great results they had gotten when they applied what I had shared with them. Many said that they felt more at peace than before we met. Several told me that when we met, they saw me as being totally peaceful. Therefore, they felt more at peace when we were together. Then it dawned me that the peace they saw was there because I no longer feared fear because of my deep faith in God. I know that I'd have the strength to handle whatever challenges I face. Please understand I still am afraid just like everyone else. But I have learned how to prevent it from mastering my life. Apparently, it shows.

One afternoon I stopped at a popular fast-food restaurant for a quick lunch before going to a business meeting. I got my food and sat down to eat while I read a book. As I sat there, I suddenly realized that someone was looking at me. I looked over at the individual, and he asked me if I was a priest or man of the cloth. I told him no. His reply was, "Then what do you do?" I told him I sold insurance part time, and I also did some life coaching. That did it. He picked up his tray and moved to my table, saying he knew that he needed to talk to me. I was somewhat taken aback, but I put my book down and began to listen.

For the next forty minutes, he shared the events in his life that were creating an enormous emotional burden. There were tears and there were smiles as he rode an emotional roller coaster. I realized after it was over that I'd completely tuned out everything around me except the man and what he was saying. I realized that I'd listened to his anguish and his hopes. I understood his fear. Then together we identified his fear. He said he understood it. Then I shared with him the definition of fear and shared some techniques for addressing it. Now he was armed with what he needed to begin working through his situation. He simply said, "Thank you so much. I really needed this." He walked out of the door with a smile on his face. As I went to my car, I realized that my shirt was wet with perspiration, and I was physically and mentally exhausted.

I thought about this encounter for several days. I shared it with Darlene, and she felt that it was just the beginning of something new in our lives. And she was so right. Finally, after a week, I needed to talk to somebody about what was happening. So, like I'd done in Boston so many years ago I went to see my priest. After I told him my background, much as I have told you in this book, I shared with him what had been happening lately. He thought for a moment and then gave me what I thought was a shocking answer.

He told me that as a priest he had seen this same thing in others but only a few times. He said because of what had gone on in my life I had somehow reached a point where people saw me differently. In other words, they saw in me God's peace and an opportunity to help them with their current situation. Moreover, they felt that I sincerely cared enough to connect with what they were feeling without being judgmental.

He told me that God has a mission for every one of us and that my mission was a "mission of presence." I asked him what that was. He explained that people are drawn to me, especially if they are experiencing emotional pain. He went on to tell me that I should always wait for them to come to me and that I shouldn't approach them. He said that when they were ready for help, they would approach me. He finished by telling me that I needed to understand that it wasn't me that was helping these people, but that it was God's message through me that was making them better.

After I left my meeting with Father, I wondered what had caused God to give me this wonderful gift. Then I thought back to what Coach shared so many years ago. I remembered him telling me about the peaceful spirit of a baby and how over the years we place shadows over our spirit and darken it. It was then that I fully realized that the spirit was the emotion of love, the spirit of God. At that moment my personal understanding of who God is became clear. To me God is that bright light I saw that evening in December 2015. I know that light is energy. So, for me God is the supreme energy source, and that energy is both intelligent as well as emotional. God is the positive energy of love. The emotion of love runs through my body; therefore, God dwells within me through the emotion of love. When I embrace that love, He gives me the strength to fight back the fear that also dwells within me. I now embrace my personal connection with Him.

We must remember that each one of those shadows we placed over our spirit pushes us one more step away from the spirit of love, which is God. At that moment, a cold chill ran down my spine as I thought back to that cold March day in Boston when I cried out for help. I realized that I had drifted away from my connection to God. I had laid so many dark shadows over my spirit that any brightness was barely visible. My spirit had gone dark. Satan had filled me with so much fear that he now had nearly complete control of my life. I only needed to look at my behavior over the past many years to confirm that statement. The wonderful thing is that energy cannot be destroyed, and that small amount that could not be consumed by fear (the portion that still connected me to God) began to fight back.

Yes, God has a sense of humor and lets us make our own decisions. Yes, we get to choose between embracing fear (Satan) or love (God). Unfortunately, as I said earlier, most of our decisions are made from fear. Therefore, many of our decisions are counter to His will. However, when we reach a point where we no longer feel that we have a connection to Him, He intervenes. We may never understand exactly how though because He works in mysterious ways. It is my opinion, however, that He will never stop fighting for us and will continually offer forgiveness if we embrace Him and have true faith in Him.

God is never dead because He is energy and energy cannot be destroyed. On that morning in Boston, He'd had enough and stepped in, for which I will always be so thankful.

Over the many years since then, I have had help in peeling away many of those dark shadows. This is why people sense God's presence when they see peace on my face. Love runs through me just as it runs through you. It does not matter how badly or undeserving you feel about yourself. Never forget that all you need to do is embrace the love within you and He will welcome you back.

Granted my spirit will never be as bright and innocent as it was when I was a baby because I will never be able to remove all the shadows. But I now understand that with the removal of each of those shadows, I move one step closer in my journey back to God, a journey that will continue until I am once again home with Him.

May God Bless you and may your journey back to Him bring you the Peace that you truly deserve.

EPILOGE

After the final edit of this book, I sent out copies to several people to get their feedback. Of course, I was very pleased that all said that they liked it and most said they couldn't put it down after they started reading it. Several, however, asked me a question I hadn't expected: why was I so open and transparent about my life, and why would I be so willing to openly share the dark side of my life and all my fear?

Now that you've read the book you may be wondering the same thing. So, let me try to explain. As I wrote in the book, you can't attain complete peace until you are willing to open your vulnerability vault. I know that may seem impossible and frightening to many. The real question is whether it is more frightening to open it up and share its contents, or to live in fear of it being discovered. It is something for each of us to ponder.

Obviously, it's a personal decision for each of us to make, which can lead to peace of mind through harmony with God and a more fulfilling life. This, of course, is why being transparent is very important. But it doesn't answer the question of why I was willing to open the vault and do it in a public forum. If I had found the peace I was seeking – and my life was better than ever – there would be no need for me to share my story with anyone other than my clients, friends, and family to help them find the peace they are seeking. That alone gives me great joy.

I believe that sharing my life story it is a part of the mission God has given me. But it goes deeper than that.

It doesn't take a genius to understand that today's world is driven by fear. Many places in the world have lived with constant fear for centuries. However, it has been different in the United States. Yes, we have experienced a level of fear as a nation, but honestly it has been a reasonability low level of fear as compared to many other places. This is because we have felt a greater level of security. Unlike many countries, we haven't experienced lengthy foreign wars on our soil. We have had a Constitution and a Bill of Rights that has protected us from the abuse of power by our leaders. We have had a justice system that has protected us through the rule of law.

Over my 76 years, I've seen an insidious, mostly unnoticed decline in the levels of these securities. The terrorist attack on 911 put a major punctuation point on the fact that our peace-loving country was vulnerable. On that day, a huge portion of our sense of security was stripped away. Unfortunately, that is not the only security that has been challenged. Our faith in our leaders, our justice system, and even in our economic system has been shaken until we find ourselves living in a culture of fear. Our world has changed drastically. That which was right fifty years ago is now wrong and what was wrong is now promoted as being right. Sadly, during this transition, we have continued to remove God from all aspects of life in the United States. In fact, the removal of God from the public forum, in my view, has contributed to the level of fear we are experiencing.

As I shared in my testimony, I slowly and methodically pulled away from God – and without realizing it – I was slowly darkening the bright spirit of God's love until I was living in almost total darkness. In my opinion, we are taking the same disastrous path as a nation. Of course, a nation does not create a culture of hate or love; it is the people who create the culture. Yes, it is true that government and media play a large role in fear mongering. But you and I are ultimately responsible for our own culture. So why would we want to create a culture of hate, prejudice, and destructive behavior? In my opinion, it was never the intention of most people to create the environment we live in today. Like myself, many have unknowingly allowed fear to overcome feelings of caring, compassion, trust, respect, and good will.

Unfortunately, when fear becomes the dominant emotion driving our decisions, we find it difficult to be understanding and respectful of those around us. One thing I learned in my journey was that I felt totally isolated once fear took over. I thought I was the only one being punished by constant challenges and heartbreaks. I had no one to put my faith and trust in. I felt that everyone else was enjoying a life of ease and enjoyment while I was left out of the mix. Because of these feelings it was easy to let fear take over. I learned, however, that fear is a very nasty and punishing taskmaster and that breaking away is a very difficult task.

It was only through the power of God's love and His blessing that I was able to break fear's hold on me enabling me to reclaim my life. I'm not certain that I have the words to express how grateful both Darlene and I are for the wonderful blessings God has bestowed upon us.

It is my deep belief that the emotion of love living within us connects us directly to God. I believe just as deeply that if we embrace that love, He will give us the power to break fear's control over us allowing us to reclaim the lives He intended for us live.

Before I go, I want to share one last thing with you. As I have said I'm Catholic. At the beginning of each new church year, we have a beautiful candlelight service. Mass is held at dusk. As parishioners enter the darkened church they receive an unlit candle. The priest says a blessing and then lights the Paschal Candle from the fire which represents the light of the world. The ushers then light a small candle from the Paschal Candle and the procession moves down the aisles of the church. The ushers light the candle of the first person in each pew as the procession moves forward. Each parishioner in turn lights the candle of the person next to him. By the time the procession has reached the front of the church, the church is bathed in a beautiful glow of candlelight. I share this with you because I believe that as we each find peace, and help one other person to find peace, the world will once again shine with the light of God's love. Here is the first verse of a beautiful song that sums it up.

"Let there be peace on earth
And let it begin with me
Let there be peace on earth
The peace that was meant to be

With God as our Father
Brothers all are we
Let me walk with my brother
In perfect harmony.

Until we are together again may God bless you and keep you.